# Tales from the Hayloft

## A Maine Farm Memoir

James E. Harris

Typesetting & Design: Carolyn H. Zukowski
Photo, back cover: Richard Harris
Town of Dayton Map: Dave Allen, www.old-maps.com

ISBN: 978-80-908094-0-6

This is a book of memoir, or what literary types call *creative non-fiction*. It's based on my present recollections of experiences growing up on a small dairy farm in Dayton, Maine, serving stateside in the US Army, entering the world of adulthood, and exploring my more mature years. I have not changed names, but may have forgotten or omitted some facts and important characters or recreated and compressed some dialogue and events. If I have offended any reader with faulty or improper recollections, I kindly recommend you write your own story.

*— James E. Harris, South Portland, Maine*

# Table of Contents

# Why Write?

Much of the farming I experienced in my early years was drudgery and involved hoeing crops to remove the energy-robbing weeds, cleaning the barn, milking cows, loading hay bales onto the wagon and stacking them away in the barn for winter feed. In the winter we cut and logged wood in the freezing cold.

I was driving a tractor by the time I was nine years old and Dad would send me out with a tractor and a rake after we harvested a field to gather the scattered hay remaining after we carried away all the bales. Later on I could operate a tractor with a mowing machine attached to mow fields of tall green grass that had matured enough to cure into hay. This was a job I loved and mastered.

I loved everything about mowing. I did it in full sunshine with fair-weather clouds skating across the sky, giving momentary relief from the heat of the sun. There was the beauty of the field ready to mow, with the breezes casting waves across the sea of grass and the ordered beauty of the neat swaths of grass laid down to cure into hay. There were always a variety of birds swooping and diving on insects stirred up by the mowing machine. And there was the intoxicating fragrance of mown hay mixed with the subtle mechanical odors of the mowing equipment.

You may wonder what this has to do with writing. Well, I am getting to that.

If you are mowing the field for the first time, walking over the field to find hidden hazards like rocks or stumps obscured in the tall grass is important. In order to mow a field of hay, you must first consider the field and its layout. Are there any trees to mow around? Are there wet areas to avoid, or a brook or ditch running through the field? What shape is the field? Square, irregular, or round? Maybe it follows a brook on one side and a wooded line or a fence on the other.

Now we are ready to mow. We mow first trip around the field clockwise because the cutter bar hangs to the right of the tractor. With the cutter bar chattering away with its knives slipping back and forth between the steel fingers of the bar, the cut hay falls backwards into a swath. Three or four turns around the field, you cut the area that the tractor drove over while cutting the first swath. We call this the back swath.

From this point on, you must be very careful not to leave any grass standing. Areas of grass standing after mowing are "holidays" and Dad would not stand for holidays in his fields. This meant that each swath had to be cut precisely, and each corner had to be turned squarely, all the while maintaining enough speed to mow the field in a timely manner. You might think that going around and around a field on a tractor would become boring. But I found it engaging as it was necessary to keep a straight line, spaced in relation to the still standing grass, watch the area ahead of the cutter to avoid hazards and to anticipate the upcoming corner in time to lift the cutter bar at the time it cleared the end of the swath. For me it became a one-car auto race, crossing the finish line at the end of the final swath.

Writing is a lot like farming. When the farmer plants a seed, he expects the seed to grow and to produce a crop, but he also knows there is a risk of failure because of the influence of many factors such as weather, pests or weeds. In the same way, the writer plants a seed, also expecting a return for the effort. Perhaps the writer only wants to express his point of view, or cannot let his story go unwritten. Maybe he wants to publish the great American novel.

Like the farmer haying a field, the writer has to survey his project, remove as many obstacles to success as possible, avoid pitfalls and hazards along the way, and keep the overall goal in mind. Sometimes the writer needs to deal with a "back swath," or include a little "back story" to make a more complete presentation.

Paragraphs must be clear and concise, like well-mowed swaths with no holidays or missing information. A writer also needs to prune, weeding out unnecessary words and phrases. Sometimes all that's needed is a bit of transplanting and nurturing, and added fertilizer and irrigation.

Why write? I think there may be as many answers to that question as there are writers. Some write to fulfill an assignment in an English class, or because their friends are doing it. Maybe it's their passion and they can't imagine their lives without it.

I'm one of those writers that had the good fortune to land in a writer's group. Writing is not my passion. It's not that thing I can't *not* do. My focus is not on being published. If that happens, I guess it would be a plus. My passion involves mechanics and solving mechanical problems.

As the saying goes, make hay while the sun shines. Now that I have time, a supportive writer's group, and a lifetime of memories to share, I think I should write them down. Maybe the generations that follow me will get a glimpse through the window into the small room that is my life.

# fire

# Dayton 1856

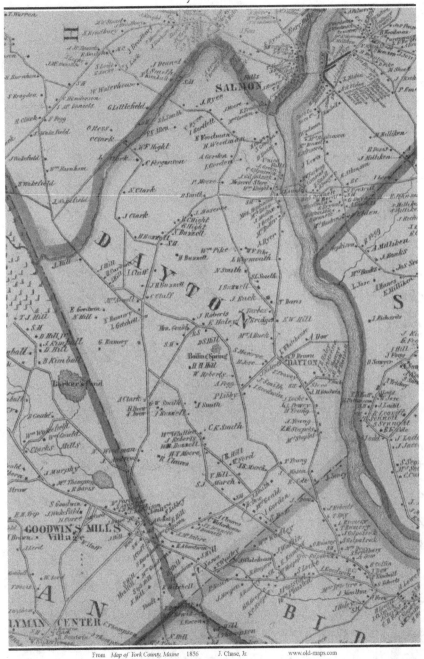

From *Map of York County, Maine* 1856    J. Chase, Jr.    www.old-maps.com

Auburn Sept 14 1891

Farther I received your
letter to Night was glad
to hear from you and to
hear that you are well
I am feeling Pritty well
I am to work Hard now
and the work will bee hard
for the next three months
I hope I Can Stand it all
right I would like to Bee up
home now and go a Gunning
for a while I hope the time
will Come again when
I Can go as i use to Go when
I was at home I received
a letter From Frank to
Night at the Same time
i received yours he Says
he has had a Bad time
with his Sister

he wonts me to come
up to Springvale to
See him next Saturday
Night I dont think I shall
bee able to he Says he
is feeling first rate now
you Stated in your letter
that you was pulling
your Beens and you Say
they are Good well i am
glad of it I may have to
Come home this winter
and help Eat them you
that Erving is with you know
well you must make him
help you get up a good
lot of wood for it is Comming
a nother Cold winter I cant
tell you when i shell Come
home I am not so far off
as i was when i was Out to
Colorado I Can Come in a very
Short time ofter i get Started
    Joseph M Burrell Park House

Auburn September 4 1891

Farther I received your letter to Night
was glad to hear from you and to hear that you are well
I am feeling Pritty well also
I am to Work Hard now and the work will bee hard for the next
three months
I hope I Can Stand it all right
I would like to Bee up home now and go a Gunning for a while
I hope the time will Come again when I can go as I use to Go
when I was at home
I received a letter From Frank to Night at the Same time i
received yours
He Sas he has had a Bad Time with his Ticka He wonts me to
Come up to Springvale to see him next Saturday night
I dont think I Shell bee able to
he Says he is feeling first rate now
you Stated in your letter that you was pulling your Beens and you
Say they are Good
well I am glad of it I may have to Come home this winter and
help Eat them
You (say) that Erving is with you know
well you must make him help you get up a good lot of wood for it
is Coming a Nother Cold winter
I cant tell you when i shell come home
I am not so far off as i was when i was out to Colorado
I Can Come in a very short time after i get started

Joseph M Buzzell, Park House Auburn

x

# Letter to Father

Many years ago, I was climbing around the attic of the cottage in the upper field of our family farm when I came across a pile of very old tools and books.

The books dated from the late 1800s and were mouse-infested, water-stained and in very poor condition. As I flipped through them, I discovered — folded into the pages of one book — a letter from a son to his father.

It was written in a very neat hand, with every letter formed in an old-fashioned calligraphy. It had no punctuation, and he misspelled many of the words with quite a few capitalized when they should have been lower-case. With no punctuation and random capitalization, it takes some studying to understand the writer's meaning.

The lack of smears or ink blotches shows that he was right-handed. I am left-handed and remember the messes I made with a fountain pen those many years ago in the one-room schoolhouse.

He was a young man but not a teenager, as he references a time in Colorado. From the tone of his letter, I would put him at between twenty-five and thirty. He seems adventurous, as evidenced by his time in Colorado and by the fact he was living in Auburn — far enough to be on his own.

He does not mention a mother in this letter. I think we can assume she is dead at the time of this writing. Maybe she died at childbirth, which was common. Or, it is possible his time out West was to visit his no-longer-spoken-about mother who perhaps ran away from the dullness of a small Maine farm in the 1800s for the excitement of the gold mines of Colorado. In those days, divorce for a woman would have been nearly impossible and for some, running away would be the only option. Maybe he didn't like the woman his mother had become and traveled back to Maine to be near his father. He has great respect for his father and is interested in his well-being.

I think his formal education stopped at about fourth grade or maybe earlier. He was drilled in the art of making letters of the alphabet, both lower- and uppercase, and he would have been introduced to spelling and making words by third grade. He didn't stay in school long enough to learn rules of grammar, including punctuation or capitalization, though he spelled "received" three times without error.

In this letter, he shows himself to be a clear thinker and an excellent communicator. I think he would have been an interesting man to know. It is a shame that we had to meet him in a dusty and dim attic so many years after he was gone.

# Lorne's Labor

He received word in the early afternoon of December 16, 1918. His brother Ben's wife, Alice, had gone into labor with her sixth pregnancy in seven years and the midwife said the baby was not positioned properly. Dr. Lorne Harris was the only doctor in the family, and Ben didn't know who else to call. In those days, women didn't give birth in the hospital, especially in poor families. Most families chose a midwife from among the experienced local women to assist with the delivery.

By the time Lorne had downed a couple of highballs to fortify himself and loaded his Chandler automobile for the trip, the weather was closing in. He had tire chains, a full tank of gasoline and a couple of extra five-gallon cans stowed on the running boards, an extra robe to ward off the cold in the unheated car and a shovel.

It was mid-afternoon when Lorne drove onto the highway and the weather had turned into snow mixed with sleet, and darkness was coming on early. By this time Alice had been in labor eight hours.

Leaving Chelmsford, Massachusetts, he found his way to US Route 1 (little more than a country road) and turned north. When he got to Hampton, New Hampshire, it was fully dark, so he stopped at an inn to rest and have a quick dinner. Before setting out from Hampton, he put on his tire chains and emptied one of his gasoline cans into the tank. The snow was building up on the road. There were no snowplows in the early twentieth century, and driving over snow-covered roads was a perilous business.

On the Hill Road in Dayton, Alice was approaching fourteen hours of painful labor. There seemed to be no progress, and the midwife was getting anxious. In Alice and Ben's bedroom was Alice, propped up with pillows, the midwife, Mrs. Hill and another local woman who helped with towels and cool water to ease the pain and wipe away the sweat. Ben and the two older boys, Bernard and John, were tormented by Alice's screams and panting, anxiously waiting for the ordeal to end. A nearby neighbor had taken in baby Eva and the two younger boys, Earl and Lyman, for the duration.

By the time the doctor arrived in Kennebunk, he had slid off the road twice. Each time he got out of the ditch by himself and back on the road. The physical effort and a couple of nips from the bottle he kept in the storage compartment under the seat helped keep him warm in his unheated automobile.

From Kennebunk, he could continue on to Biddeford and then travel up the River Road to Ben's farm on the Hill Road in Dayton, or he could take what is now State Route 35 to Goodwins Mills and across the Waterhouse Road to the Hill Road. He had been on the road for a long time and was tired, but after a couple more nips, he decided on route 35. The road from Kennebunk to Goodwins Mills is a twisty road even today, but back then with the weather, lack of lighting and a gravel and dirt surface, it was nasty. By then the snow was about a foot deep and the edges of the road indistinct.

Two or three miles out of Kennebunk, the road takes a dip and a quick right turn. It was there that the car slid completely off the road into a deep ditch. The doctor was having second thoughts about this trip as he trudged back to a house he had seen about a quarter mile before with its lights on. He roused the farmer, who agreed to harness his team and pull the car back onto the road. Three hours later, with the front bumper pulled away from the right front wheel, and after declining the farmer's offer to stay for the night, Lorne was back on the road.

It was now well after midnight and being extra careful, Lorne continued on to Goodwins Mills where he arrived, nearly out of gas, at daybreak. Rousing Ray Burbank at his gas station, he could fill his tank before attempting the final two-and-a-half miles to Ben's farm. The last lap of the journey seemed to take forever as he had to push forward as far as he could go in the deep snow, then stop and back up before taking another run at it.

Finally arriving at the foot of the Hill Road and realizing he couldn't possibly drive his car up the steep hill to Ben's farm, the doctor grabbed his medical bag and trudged the last quarter mile to his destination.

Alice was twenty-four hours in labor by the time Lorne arrived. Throwing off his snow-covered coat and hat, and saying a quick hello to Ben, he rushed in to see his patient. By now, her screams and panting had reduced to low moans and shallow breaths. A quick examination confirmed his worst fears. Alice had lost too much blood and was weak and fading, and the baby was showing no signs of life.

Alice and her baby girl died that day in the early afternoon, leaving Ben with five youngsters to raise on his hardscrabble farm.

Later on, after the funeral and when things had settled down a little, Ben decided that two-year-old Eva would live with Lorne and his wife in Massachusetts, and Lyman and Earl would live with a local school teacher. Bernard and John stayed on the farm as Bernard was the oldest boy and John could cook.

All four boys grew up and had farms. Bernard had the family farm on the Hill Road, my dad John had the Buzzell Road farm (now known as Harris Farm), Lyman farmed on the Hill Road in Lyman, and Earl had a farm outside Gorham. John and Lyman were successful farmers; the other two, not so much. Earl married three times and left two families of children behind when he died of complications due to lack of medical care.

Ben never remarried, and he lived a bitter existence until he died in his late sixties.

Baby Eva grew up to become the lovely daughter Doctor Lorne and his wife could never have.

# Buzzell Road

My first memory of Buzzell Road is of a one-lane dirt road comprising two wheel tracks with green grass growing between them. It was 1945 and my family was moving into a two-car garage Dad and some friends had built after a fire had leveled our home on the Waterhouse Road.

For the next eight years, my family turned the old Buzzell farm into a working farm. Set onto a concrete foundation that Dad had built, our new house had two bedrooms across the rear and a great room across the front to serve as a kitchen and dining area with a cast-iron sink and a wood-burning Glenwood kitchen stove. An abbreviated wall separated the kitchen area from the living room. Our bathroom was a two-hole outhouse in the nearby barn.

A windmill pumped water from a spring in the woods two hundred yards away. The spring was not on our property, but water rights went with our deed. The windmill pumped from the spring to a water tower next to our barn. One cow requires over twenty gallons of water per day to produce milk. When we moved to the new farm, there was no electricity, so we lived a cold water existence for a couple of years. We heated Saturday night bath water on the wood stove. Baths were in a galvanized tub in front of the wood stove in the kitchen. We drew lots to determine who would get "first bath" with clean water.

The original house on the Buzzell farm had burned some years before, leaving part of the attached woodshed and a crooked one-hundred foot barn. Over the next fifteen years, my dad, along with the labor of some hired help and me and my two brothers, straightened the barn and replaced floor timbers. We poured a full-length concrete foundation and installed a tie-up for sixty cows in the basement. During that time we also cut enough timber to provide all the lumber to build a five-bedroom house to replace the one that had burned years before.

Next door was a single-family house used by the town of Dayton as a poorhouse. It had a shed and attached outhouse and was occupied by different families over the years. First were the Edgecombs, an elderly couple. After the Edgecombs came "Babe" and his family. Babe made what living he could as a fishmonger. I remember he had a pickup truck with a wooden bed to hold ice and a cabinet for the fish he sold door-to-door. Mom would often end up buying some of his leftover fish for our dinner. It was much later in my life that I found out what fresh fish tasted like.

Then there was a family who had a son Joey with whom we played cars and trucks on a dirt pile behind the barn, and another family who had a daughter about my age. After that, the town decided not to have a poorhouse and my dad and mom bought that house with the acre of land and used it to provide housing for the hired man and his wife who came to work on the farm in 1949.

At the far side of a large open field southwest from our house lay the Mullet farm. There was a dirt lane that connected that farm with the Buzzell Road and to the Hollis Road, which is now Route 35.

The Mullet farm had a farmhouse and a barn with the usual complement of outhouse and machinery sheds. Old Mr. Mullet kept a dozen cows for milking, a few hens in a coop to produce eggs for sale, and grew strawberries and sweet corn in the summer. They separated the cream from part of their milk and made butter to sell as well. The balance of their milk production went to Landry's Dairy for processing for their home delivery service. I remember Old Joe Mullet as a contrary man with little good to say about anyone or anything, and his son Joe was quite a lot like him. Younger Joe and his wife and three children lived in a small house on the Waterhouse Road, near our first small farm. Although he had a factory job in Biddeford, Joe traveled to his father's farm every day to help him until he died.

Young Joe took over the Mullet farm, sold the house on the Waterhouse Road and moved his family onto Mullet's lane. Soon after that Joe sold the old Silver King tractor and bought a new Farmall Super C, row crop tractor. Joe was a fanatic about Boston baseball, both the Braves and the Red Sox, and was also a bedrock Republican. He would walk across the field to pass the time with Dad on a Saturday afternoon. I can still hear him complaining about whatever that "God-damned Truman" had done. Joe was a slender man and not very tall. He was always the umpire for the town baseball games, and when he came over to talk, he always stood with his hands on his knees in an umpire stance.

Traveling southeast down Buzzell Road, the next property belonged to the Gregoire family. It consisted of a farmhouse with a shed and a detached barn. It had been an active farm at one time, but most of the farmland was sold or had grown up to bushes. Mr. Gregoire worked in town. They had one son and at least four younger daughters. As they were Catholic, we did not socialize with them except at school and town functions. Looking back on it, I am sorry that we were not friendlier to the Gregoire family. The girls were smart and quite pretty, but shy, and I suppose their parents warned them about being involved with Protestants as much as my parents warned us about being involved with Catholics.

Just beyond the Gregoire family was a two-family house occupied by Mary Waterhouse, who owned the property, and Virginia Gay, Mary's cousin. Mrs. Gay was a widow with four children, the oldest a boy, John, followed by a girl, Mary, and two younger boys, Fred and Amos. Our common neighborhood encompassed over a mile from end to end, and the eight of us — my two brothers and I, the three Gay boys and the two Mullet boys — became fast friends. We were always ready to get into mischief together and always up for a an impromptu game of scrub baseball or football. We explored the forests, built forts, climbed trees, played army games and cowboys and Indians.

Just on the other side of the hill from the Waterhouse/Gay property lived the Ring family. I'm not sure what the Ring parents were like, because we almost never saw them. They didn't go to church, and they kept to themselves. Their poorly constructed home had no outbuildings. It was in a little clearing beside the road, surrounded by woods on three sides. They had three very shy children — two boys and a girl.

All the children I have mentioned attended the one-room schoolhouse at the intersection of Buzzell Road and the Waterhouse Road. Mrs. Gay was our teacher in those years and the school contained all eight grades. The building still stands and is now a museum. There were desks for about thirty students. A black cast- iron stove provided all the heat for the school. In the winter we would toast our lunch sandwiches on the red-hot stove. More than once a student would leave a sandwich on the stove too long and it filled the room with smoke. During freezing winter weather, the Mother's Club members took turns bringing a hot lunch for everyone at the school — a soup or stew or a large casserole with homemade bread or rolls.

The town supplied and stocked a woodshed outside. The teacher handled curriculum for all eight grades and had to start the fire in the stove early enough to warm the building by nine o'clock when classes started. She also had to maintain order and discipline, and I doubt she was paid more than forty dollars per week. There was a double two-hole outhouse at the rear of the building, one side for girls and one side for boys, accessible from inside the classroom.

Buzzell Road was typical of the roads in Dayton, Maine, in the forties. There were four one-room schools. Most of the roads were dirt except for the Hollis road and the New County Road, now Rt. 35 and Rt. 5. In those days there were twenty or twenty-five active small dairy farms in the town with ten to twenty cows each. There were two commercial dairies — Cole Farm Dairy and Landry's Dairy — and the farmers trucked their milk daily to the dairy. Before electricity came to the farms, they kept milk cold in coolers chilled by block ice cut in the winter from the mill pond and stored in ice houses covered by hay or sawdust.

When new sanitation laws required farms to convert to bulk milk handling, it spelled the end for small family dairies. The laws required even the smallest farm to invest three- to five-thousand dollars for a stainless steel bulk tank and a sanitary milk house. Today, the only active dairy in Dayton is the Harris Farm — the farm where I grew up. It has doubled in size to about seven hundred acres and owes its success to keeping up with modern technology, diversification, dedication and hard work.

The dirt road I remember from 1945 is now a broad, paved, two-lane country road, as are most of the roads in town. Most of the open agricultural fields are grown up to bushes on the way to returning to forest land or boast new, upscale homes with paved driveways and manicured lawns. Many of the old dairy barns are still standing beside restored and upgraded farmhouses, the barns themselves re-sided and re-roofed for new lives as workshops, storage spaces, and other commercial functions.

At a recent Thornton Academy senior reunion, I sat at lunch with Fred Gay, my best friend from grammar school and as we talked and reminisced, it was like slipping back into one of those fourth-grade desks in that one-room schoolhouse.

# Sap Camp

It was a time of sweetness. When thirsty, we drank the fresh cool sap from buckets hanging from maple trees. During the boiling, we sampled the mixture as it matured. Later, we tasted the finished syrup, dropped on clean snow. The solidified maple candy had the intense flavor of the maple with a smoky undertone.

Sugaring started in late February and lasted until the weather warmed in the first weeks of April. It was a thrilling time for a five-year-old boy, as maple sugar season signaled the first hint of spring. Snow was melting as warm days followed wintry nights.

The building we called "Sap Camp" was a hip-roofed, one-car garage that Dad had moved to the top of a small hill overlooking the farm and next to a lane that led into the maple orchard. Snuggled in among the maples with the two swing-doors overlooking the meadow, it was a pleasant place to spend an afternoon of tending the fire and sampling the emerging sweet syrup.

We carried sap from the tapped maple trees to the camp in five-gallon buckets and poured it into two pans arranged in tandem over the stone arch Dad had built. Once we had collected enough sap and the pans were about half full, we built a fire in the fire pit. Soon billows of sweet-smelling steam mixed with smoke from the fire would rise from the two pans and fill the camp with a smoky-sweet aroma.

There was constant activity at the sap camp during the time the trees were producing. We maintained the fire under the pans at just the right temperature to keep the sap boiling, but not hot enough to burn the sweet syrup that was emerging. The pan over the fire boiled the hardest while the rear pan replenished it. We would then refill the rear pan with fresh sap from the trees. It took a lot of wood to reduce forty gallons of sap to a gallon of syrup. We dragged wood from the pile, bucksawed it and split it with an axe to fit the length of the fire pit.

It was always late in the evening when we had finished barn chores and supper. We enjoyed staying up late in that old sap camp lit by a kerosene lantern and the glow from the fire pit under the pans. We reduced the fire as we brought the syrup to a finish, then dipped and filtered it into gallon tin jugs with screw-on caps.

Our young family was trying to eke out a living while developing a farm. The added income from seventy or eighty gallons of maple syrup at five-dollars a gallon paid for the fertilizer and seed for the summer crops. Dad did all the hard work in the early years. We boys were young and didn't know about hard times.

When we were older, I and my two brothers would experience aching muscles from carrying buckets of sap from the far reaches of the maple orchard. I guess it was then that we realized — our teamwork was part of the sweetness.

# The Great Fire of 1947

It's the fear that I remember most. The fear that inhabits a child whose parents are afraid. In October 1947, the Great Forest Fire swept a path of destruction across Maine's York County. Only three years earlier, my family had lost everything but our lives in a fire that destroyed our house and barn.

After the fire on Waterhouse Road in 1944, my parents built a 24' by 24' building for temporary shelter, which they moved onto a foundation on Buzzell Road when that 300 acre property became available. After two-and-a-half years of very hard work we had electricity, a refrigerator, an electric powered milk cooler, electric lights in the barn, and an electric milking machine. No more cutting and storing ice and no more kerosene lanterns to milk by. We had a windmill and water tower. We had a mismatched team of horses, a tractor that was half Model A Ford and half Fordson tractor, and a '36 Ford dump truck.

The idea of losing everything to fire once again must have been unbearable and unthinkable. The fire had been sweeping in our direction all week and we could see the red-orange flames in the distance as dry pine trees burst into fire. It darkened the sky like an evening at noontime, and the acrid smell of burning pine was always there. Mom and Dad sent us three boys to stay with neighbors who lived in a house surrounded by open fields. This would be safer than at home, surrounded by woods on three sides. I had to share a bed with a boy my age who wet the bed most nights.

17

When the danger of fire lessened, they brought us back home to a surreal scene. They had backed the '36 Ford dump truck up to the side of the milkroom hitched to a chain which went through a hole in the wall and surrounded the milk cooler. They filled the truckbed with most of our household goods. If the fire got too close, the plan was to pull the milk cooler into the yard and drive the truckload of household goods to safety. Using the water tower, they wet down the grass around the barn and also wet down the house, barn and shed roofs in case of flying embers.

In a few days, the fire danger passed, and even though the fire had approached our land in several places, it never got over three feet inside our property line. Mom attributed this to her constant prayers. She allowed that Dad's going without sleep and patrolling the property for thirty-six hours may have also had something to do with it.

In the following years we heard many stories about the Great Fire of '47 — many sad, some humorous, and some outlandish. It destroyed many farms along with entire communities. The fire consumed thousands of acres of forest. There was a story of a fireball that flew across the length of my uncle's farm, crossing the Saco River and setting fire to the woods. The Board of Selectmen of the Town of Dayton decided that it was dangerous to leave the new Walters Snowfighter snowplow truck in the wooden town shed lest the shed catch fire. So they parked it outside on the street. The fire didn't touch the shed, but it destroyed the new truck parked on the street.

After they officially extinguished the fire, its aftermath was everywhere. Chimneys stood tall against the sky where farmhouses once stood. Tall pines stripped black against the horizon. The shape of the land, once obscured by lush forest and undergrowth, was laid bare and ugly. A Sunday country drive, one of Dad's favorite activities, was no longer beautiful but a bleak trip through despair.

Over the next few years, green returned as new grass emerged and bushes sprouted among the dead and dying trees. Logging companies flourished as they salvaged and milled trees for lumber that went into the construction of replacement buildings. Government agencies were on the scene with free military housing — brownish-green, military-colored, metal, bolted-together huts that some families lived in for the next twenty years. I think those are mostly gone by now, some converted into chicken houses or garages.

Seventy years have passed since the Great Fire, and only a handful of people who fought the fires are still alive. But the lessons learned as a result of the fire are clear all around us. Remember, there was a time when a town fire department would only go as far as the town line and watch a property over the line burn to the ground. Changes in woodland management, building codes and communication and dispatching cooperation between neighboring towns has all grown out of these lessons.

In our family, the fear of fire had a significant effect on the way we lived and worked. Dad never burned brush or trash unless it was a rainy day. He wouldn't allow anyone in the barn with a cigarette or pipe. He always contracted out electrical work to a licensed electrician to reduce the chance of an electrical fire. Fear of that orange yellow glow in the sky is one significant factor in the continued existence of the farm Dad and Mom started over seventy years ago.

# Roy's Garage

The smoke from Biddeford's burning dump constantly shrouded Roy's Garage at the intersection of South Street. I don't remember what brand of gasoline they sold there — maybe ESSO or Shell — but I remember Raymond Roy. Throughout my childhood and early adulthood, his was the "go to" place for gasoline, inspection stickers and the occasional candy bar. Even though he had a first name, we always called him Roy. He was probably is his late thirties when I first encountered him, though we weren't properly introduced because I was just an eight-year-old kid in a pickup truck and Roy was dealing with my dad.

Roy was impressive to me. He was medium height and sturdy with a tendency toward what we would now call a "beer gut." I didn't know about beer back then coming from a family of non-drinkers. He had one withered arm that crookedly hung from his shoulder with a misshapen hand, and he had a wide toothy grin with one gold tooth among the others in his upper jaw. On Roy's head was a greasy leather short-billed hat, and on his upper lip a pencil-thin mustache. He could hold his cigarette in the withered hand while he pumped gasoline with his good hand.

His office was a treasure trove of items and odors — with shelves of knickknacks, candies and gaskets with fan belts hanging on the walls. Behind the register, he guarded packs of tobacco and bottles of beer. The air smelled of cigar smoke and oiled wood floor. These odors were exotic and wonderful to a boy from a dairy farm where clean air was tainted with the odor of cow manure and souring milk.

Running the length of the building was the single service bay with the workbench along one side and an air compressor. Set into the floor was a concrete-lined pit about five feet deep for servicing cars from underneath. If your car needed an oil change, grease job or exhaust work, you would drive into the service bay straddling the pit and Roy would climb under to do the work.

In the lot behind the garage, Roy had a small junkyard filled with old cars he salvaged for customers who needed an economical repair to "get by." He also parked his battered Chevrolet wrecker with the hand-crank winch in the back lot. The back lot bordered the agricultural field of the town poorhouse — a farm between Roy's Garage and the town dump.

Some years later, in my late twenties and back for a summer visit, I drove by the area. The burning dump was closed. The town's poorhouse was closed and demolished. The town had built about fifty low-income housing units and Roy's garage, a victim of the times where oil companies gobbled each other up and imposed a corporate image that didn't include mom-and-pop filling stations, was closed. On that hot summer day, I could still sense a hint of dump smoke, gasoline, and oiled wood floor.

# Billy and the Bull

Of course Mom and Dad had warned my younger brother —
don't go into the field where the bull is, but my little brother Billy
was intent on filling his bag with hickory nuts.

It was late summer, and the nuts had been falling from the lone
hickory tree in that field where the bull was grazing in the lush
grass. Hickory nuts look and taste like a smaller version of
walnut, and it takes a lot of them to amount to anything. Maybe
Billy was thinking of bringing the nuts to Mom so she could
make some of her delicious nut muffins, or maybe he just wanted
to have a stash of his own to eat.

The bull was a mature animal with an unpredictable disposition.
Bulls rarely like to be messed with, and they take umbrage when
people enter their space. He probably didn't seem too big a threat
to my brother.

Billy decided those nuts were worth the risk, so he sauntered into
the field. When he got to the hickory tree, the bull lifted his head
in interest. But interest soon turned to anger, and the bull started
walking toward the tree, head and horns lowered at the intruder.
As the walk turned into a trot, Billy recognized his predicament.
The fence and safety were too far away, and the bull was picking
up speed.

Billy hid behind the hickory tree, but the bull circled around.
Soon they were both running around the tree. Billy was in pretty
good shape for a six-year-old, but he soon realized that he
couldn't keep outrunning a full-grown bull. He had to do
something, and soon.

There was no chance for Billy to climb to safety as there were no low branches on the tree. His only chance was to make it somehow to the fence. After what seemed like the hundredth circle, Billy made a run for it, tossing over his bag of nuts to safety. When he got to the fence and under it, he looked back and saw the angry bull still circling the tree, snorting indignantly.

# Under a Winter Moon

It was cold. A brilliant full moon cast a long shadow from the gigantic lone elm near the edge of the forty-acre meadow. Several heavy snows, a day or so of mild weather, a day of cold rain followed by the severe cold snap had produced a glittering, icy crust strong enough for a grown man to walk on.

It was late January 1951, after my tenth birthday. Winter was long and boring on the isolated farm that year, with snow on the ground from early November. Cabin fever was setting in after a week of no school because of the snow and ice storms.

We milked the cows, fed the calves and watered their pens. We pitched hay down from the loft to feed the cows when they finished their grain and silage. We spread fresh dry sawdust on the cow stalls for bedding, which gave the barn a pleasant pine smell. We lifted the ten gallon cans of milk into the cooler, rinsed the milking machines and put them away on the racks in the milk room.

It was a treat to return to the house where Mom tended our supper over the cast-iron stove after the chill in the barn and the cold of the outdoors. In our converted two-car garage of a house, that stove provided the only heat. Later in the evening, the house would cool as the fire burned low. Dad or Mom would get up several times during the night to feed the fire and keep away the bitter cold.

After supper, Dad went out to the barn to push the last of the hay into the mangers and check the barn while we three boys listened to a radio show or read books like *Little Joe Otter* or *Reddy Fox* while Mom finished with the dishes. When Dad came in from the barn that night, he asked us if we'd like to go sliding.

Dad would surprise us every once in a while. Sometimes on a wintry Sunday afternoon he would take us on a long walk through the woods behind the barn to Clarence's pond for an afternoon of ice skating.

The moon had risen, and the night was perfect for sliding. Deep crusty snow drifted and hardened into flats and moguls, hard enough to support our sleds and sleek enough to speed us on our way down the hills and across the meadow. It bridged over the brooks and the fences, enabling us to glide a half mile.

We coasted our sleds until we could go no further and then climbed the nearest incline and slid back across the great meadow. Tired and chilled to the bone, we made our way back to the house over gleaming snow under a moon so bright we needed no other light. Mom had kept the wood stove blazing hot with tea and cocoa ready.

# Christmas Ice

Christmas Day that year dawned clear, with no snow on the ground. Deep cold had paved all the ponds with clear ice perfect for skating.

We were out of bed extra early that morning and dressed in a hurry so we could open our Christmas stockings before barn chores. I wondered how Santa could deliver our presents as we had no fireplace and no chimney other than a pipe leading from our kitchen stove. My questions were short-lived as the proof was right in front of me — presents under the tree and a stocking full of goodies hanging by the stove.

Like farm kids everywhere, we three boys understood that presents had to wait until we did chores and settled the cows for the day. By 7:30 we had milked and fed the cows, dusted the trenches with superphosphate, spread fresh bedding and swept the walkways. We then traipsed into the house ready for breakfast and some Christmas tree action. Dad always took what seemed like an hour of extra time in the barn on Christmas morning. By the time he returned to the house, ate breakfast and lingered over his tea, our anxiety level was at a fever pitch and we were bouncing off the walls.

Every year Mom and Dad designated one of us boys with the great honor of being Santa's helper who would pass out one present at a time to each family member. There weren't a lot of store-bought presents in those years. We could expect Mom's hand knit socks and sweaters, one or two toys for each boy and always a new hand-knit red sweater vest for Dad. That year we each got used skates from the secondhand store in Biddeford. Dad had sharpened the blades on his grind wheel in the farm workshop.

With presents opened and gift wrappings folded and put away by 9:00 o'clock, we had three hours of free time until we had to be at the annual family gathering at Whippoorwill Poultry Farm, which belonged to Uncle Morris. Dad suggested ice skating at Clarence's pond, which could be reached by walking across our fields and through the woods.

The pond covers about an acre and was formed by damming the brook with stone at some point in the late 1800s. When we arrived that day with Dad we found it smooth and glittering in the sun.

Dad surprised us with his love of ice skating. He skated forward and backward, made figure eights and cut circles. Then he built up speed and jumped over a log that extended onto the ice. Then he took some time to show us how to push off and glide, how to turn and how to stop.

This was our first time on real skates, and while we weren't hockey team material in one day, we learned to not fear the ice and how to skid into a stop. We made our way to Clarence's pond many days that winter and many winters after.

# Great-Aunt Nellie

Great-aunt Nellie came to stay with us during Christmas each year. She was my mother's aunt and sister to my grandmother, who had died of consumption shortly after raising her four children. By the time I was old enough to be aware of her, she was in her sixties, short and stout, and with her silver hair tightly permed and rimless spectacles she looked very much the part of the retired schoolteacher. She had a comfortable pension, an opinion about everything, and an expectation that people would respect and comply with her opinions and demands.

A few days before Christmas, Great-aunt Nellie would arrive by bus in Biddeford, which was about five miles away. She usually would stay overnight at the Thatcher Hotel and telephone our house in the morning asking for someone to come for her. After we had finished morning chores, Dad would drive to Biddeford with the red 1948 Ford pickup truck to transport Aunt Nellie to the farm.

Dad and Aunt Nellie tolerated each other. I'm pretty sure that she had made it quite clear in the past that Dad was not deserving of her favorite niece. She always insisted on spending the Christmas season at our farm in our tiny house that had only three rooms and no bathroom, while Mom's two sisters lived close by, with large houses and plenty of rooms and flush toilets.

Aunt Nellie always arrived with two suitcases. One case had her clothing for the visit and she filled the other with gifts, one for each member of our family, including Dad.

In our living room was a piano, one straight-backed and two upholstered chairs, a rocker and a couch that folded down to make an uncomfortable bed. On her Christmas visits, Aunt Nellie slept on the foldout bed and in the mornings after Dad had gone to the barn to do the milking, we three boys would jump into bed with Aunt Nellie and she would tell us her original stories.

Even though Mom read bedtime stories to us every night, Aunt Nellie's stories were special and often held a lesson that even though individuals had differing ideas and opinions, they could get along and be respectful to one another. Many of her stories featured animals in desperate situations. I remember one story in particular where a cat got stuck following a mouse because the mouse had cut off the cat's whiskers while the cat was sleeping and the cat didn't realize the tunnel was too narrow. Through this story we learned that cats judge the size of an opening with their whiskers.

We were blessed to grow up in a time when Christmas was more of a holy celebration that held the promise of better times for the world. It was a time of skating parties followed by hot cocoa at the church or someone's house. It was a time when we caroled from farm to farm then returned to a warm, pine-scented gathering place for a Christmas party with games, bobbing for apples and more carol singing.

On Christmas Eve, there was always a service at the village church and more caroling for the youth group and young adults. Then home to bed and the promise of wonderful gifts in the morning.

There was so much activity and anticipation — perhaps a bit like the time of the original nativity when the world awaited the Promised One.

# earth

# Cattle Dealers

"The only reason I am offerink you thirty-five dollars for this worn out old cow is because I like you." Mr. Niemann, the cattle dealer, has arrived at our farm just at milking time. He and Dad have already been about a half hour into negotiating.

The duel had started with Dad offering the cow to Mr. Niemann for seventy-five dollars, take it or leave it. During the first half hour of haggling, Dad strode out into the main floor of the barn to pitch down some hay for the cows and pushed the rest of the corn silage into the mangers. When Dad returned to the tie-up where the negotiations were taking place, Mr. Niemann stepped out to his old green rattletrap cattle truck where his son was patiently waiting. He backed the truck out of the driveway as if to leave the negotiations altogether. After a moment or so he drove back into the barnyard, got out of his truck and reentered the tie-up.

"I vill make you one last offer of forty dollars because we have been friends a very long time," says Mr Niemann.

"I can let you have her for sixty," says Dad, "otherwise she will stay in the barn. Maybe the Bragdons will give me what she is worth. And Chasse over in Sanford is always looking for an old cow to put into hamburg."

This bickering went on for about another half hour until both parties had agreed at fifty dollars. Once they struck a deal, they lost no further time getting the old cow out of the barn and up the steep ramp into the truck.

We regularly dealt with three or four cattle dealers who made the rounds to all the local farmers. There were the Bragdon brothers from South Berwick who were most interested in "vealers" — young calves fed only milk and no grain until they were big enough to slaughter for high-priced veal. Then there was Mr. Chasse in Sanford who owned a slaughterhouse and made just about everything into ground hamburger. And of course Mr. Niemann, who wanted nothing to do with distressed cows and mostly sold into the Brighton market.

Of these three, I'm pretty sure Dad got more enjoyment from dealing with Mr. Niemann. I'm convinced that both of them knew at the outset when Mr. Niemann offered twenty-five and Dad asked for seventy-five, at the end of the game they would load the cow into the truck for fifty. They had to play the game and do the dance. It was a ritual and entertainment, and it always ended with a sense of accomplishment and completion.

# Mom and the Tractor

It's the first of July 1950, and the weather is good for haying — bright sun during the day and dry nights. Most of the first crop of hay is in the barn, and we have mowed the final ten acres to rake and gather into windrows. Using a truck with a hayrack and towing the hay-loader, we load the loose hay and bring it to the barn for storage in the haymows and scaffolds.

Once the load arrives at the barn, we lift the hay into the barn using a system of ropes and pulleys. We call this operation "pulling off the hay." Some farmers would use a well-trained horse that understands voice commands; others use a pickup truck or a tractor to pull the rope.

A good farmer aims to have the first crop of hay under cover by the fourth of July. With time running short and a threat of wet weather in the forecast, Dad is feeling the stress. Short on crew, he presses Mom into driving the 1947 Ford tractor to pull the hay. Mom doesn't like to drive the tractor, but she's willing to help.

For most of the day, things go smoothly until about two in the afternoon. As Mom backs up, being careful not to drive into the rope, she maneuvers to where she can park the tractor until she can pull the next load. When she steps on the brake, her foot slips off the clutch pedal and the tractor hits the side of the woodshed, moving it off its foundation. Dad says a few words that might be better left unsaid. Mom gets indignant and heads to the kitchen with tears in her eyes and I get an immediate promotion to tractor driver — a position I hold for the rest of the harvest.

Many years later, I visited Mom, who was lying in a hospital bed for the last time. She had survived a heart attack and breast cancer and was very hard of hearing and blind. I asked her if she remembered backing the tractor into the woodshed. She laughed with a twinkle in her dull blue eyes. "Yeah, but I never had to drive that tractor again, did I?"

Until that moment, I had never considered that maybe it wasn't an accident.

# Cows in the Corn

I was eleven years old, and it was my turn to stay home and mind the three-hundred-acre farm with thirty-five cows while my family left for the afternoon to do shopping and other errands. They wouldn't be home until nightfall. My jobs while they were away included sweeping up the barn, putting fresh sawdust in all the stalls, laying superphosphate in the trench behind the cows to discourage the flies, water the garden (making sure to turn off the hose before it got too wet) and keep a close eye on the cows grazing in an area surrounded by a temporary electric fence next to the two-acre field of sweet corn just out of sight of the barnyard.

It was a scorching afternoon with no breeze to provide relief. The barn was about three-quarters full of fragrant first crop packed loose in the haymow. I had checked on the cows once in the early afternoon and they were secure and grazing on lush, ankle-deep second crop. After finishing all the other chores, a nap in the hay mow seemed in order.

I don't know how long I slept, but when I awoke I felt that something wasn't right. I had finished with barn chores and I turned the water off at the faucet. It had been a while since I had checked the cows, so I trudged up the hill to look. What I found when I got to the top of the hill caused me to wail in total frustration.

The cows had broken through the electric fence and all thirty-five were milling through the two-acre corn field, munching with wild abandon. Cows are eating machines. They will eat standing up, lying down, walking and even running. What they like to eat most in all the world is corn — grain corn, silage corn, dry corn, or wet corn. But they especially love sweet corn in a field that is almost ready to harvest. Once in a cornfield, up to their necks in the food they love the most, it is next to impossible to drive them out. But that is what I had to do, all by myself, without even a dog to help me.

I can't tell you every move I made to accomplish getting the cows back into the grass field. I can tell you it involved a lot of running and hollering as some cows I had evicted from the corn made their way back in as I drove another group out. But they are by nature herd animals, and once I had about a third of them back into the grass field, the rest were easier to move. Eventually, I had them all out of the corn and the fence repaired.

Exhausted as I was, I spent the rest of the afternoon patrolling the fence between the corn and the grass until it was time to lead them to the barn for their evening milking.

The next day, Dad noticed cow tracks in the cornfield and asked if the cows had gotten out. I told him that some of them had gotten into the corn, but I had taken care of it.

# The Bull That Soared

By the time Gregory arrived on the hill overlooking our farmyard, he had already experienced an eventful morning. As a now mature, fifteen-month-old bull, he had been introduced to the heifers at his home farm and today he was eager to expand his horizons.

Earlier on that fine June morning, he learned the gate on his pen was not securely fastened and so he had strolled out into the barnyard. Already in an adventuresome mood, he made his way to the edge of the field and entered the woods between his home and the neighboring farm.

The woods were dark and thick, and Gregory had to find his way around fallen trees and thick clumps of bushes. He came to a meandering brook and stopped for a long cool drink before continuing his journey. When he came out of the wooded area, he was confronted with a broken-down barbed wire fence he could cross without difficulty. Moving into the open field of the neighbor's farm, he could just see the top of the barn. When he got to the top of the hill, he could make out the barnyard area where several young heifers were grazing.

Bulls, especially young bulls, are not deep thinkers. And in the presence of pretty young heifers their judgment gets a little clouded. Young Gregory continued into the barnyard area without a backward glance.

I was about twelve years old at the time this strange dark bull ambled into the barnyard. I was doing barn chores, cleaning up the area around the back of the barn near the silo.

Our barn was large, a hundred feet long, and as was typical for most New England dairy barns, built on a slope. It was three stories high at the front entrance with a large, sliding door for entrance to the main floor. From the rear it was four stories high. So, looking at the front of the barn, one would see the ground floor as the main floor and from the rear of the barn the main floor was actually the second floor that overlooked the rear barnyard. As it was a nice June day, the rear barn door was open for ventilation.

Gregory was loping with enthusiasm by now and was approaching his anticipated liaison with the heifers who were grazing in the field. Foreseeing what was about to happen, I raised the alarm and soon Dad and Danny, our hired man, appeared along with my older brother, Art. The three of them soon steered Gregory toward the front of the barn. Their intent was to drive him onto the main floor of the barn and shut the door so he could not escape. Mr. Meserve, who owned Gregory, would come and take him home on a lead. Gregory entered the barn on the main floor as planned, and Dad closed the door, trapping the young bull inside.

Gregory, however, had other ideas. He could see the open door one hundred feet away at the end of the barn. With the sun streaming in, it looked like freedom. Gregory ran toward that rectangle of daylight.

A young bull can put up quite a burst of speed in a short distance.

I had remained outside at the rear of the barn, and could hear hoofbeats approaching. I had my eyes on that second-story back door and watched in awe as Gregory leaped out through the door and took flight. Flying, Gregory remained upright, but his glide angle was pretty steep. He soon landed sprawled on all fours. It took a few seconds for Gregory to recover from his landing as he picked himself up off the ground on unsteady legs, apparently none the worse for wear.

The last I saw Gregory, he was hightailing it home, making excellent speed over the hill.

# Batter Up

Joe Mullett, a small wiry man in his mid-forties, with graying dark hair peeking out from under his baseball cap and a protective face mask, is the Norman Rockwell equivalent of a small town sandlot umpire. He peers over the shoulder of Donald Waterhouse, the catcher, toward Jamie Waterhouse, the pitcher. In an umpire's crouch, one hand with splayed fingers to count balls and the other clutching the ever-present Camel cigarette and counting strikes, Joe is ready for anything on the field.

Jamie and Donald are brothers, Jamie's the oldest and always the pitcher. The two boys are the two central figures on our town team. Donald is quite tall and slender and would like to pitch, but his dominant older brother controls their relationship. Besides, Donald's only ball glove is a catcher's mitt and Jamie has the fielder's glove. Jamie is several years older than most of the players and is the de facto coach and team front office. He schedules the games between the several town teams in the area.

It is a warm summer evening, we've finished our chores, and it will be a couple of hours before it is too dark to see the ball. There is a growl of thunder off to the west and a couple of dark clouds on the horizon.

Tonight we are playing a team from Waterboro — they arrive in a rusty red old GMC pickup truck with some players packed into the cab while the rest ride on the bed. Their truck kicks up a cloud of dust that mixes with their smoking exhaust and drips oil and antifreeze onto the gravel parking lot.

We make our teams from whatever players are available that evening. One has a uniform shirt with a Red Sox logo across the back and a player's name above the pocket, another has a Braves baseball cap. Most are in clothes straight from chores with barn smells and stains. Several of the boys on each team have high-top sneakers, some have work shoes, otherwise known as clodhoppers, and some even have baseball shoes with cleats. The one common thread that connects us is that we are all here to play baseball.

We have to decide who gets to bat first. Jamie tosses a bat to the other manager who catches it, and fist over fist they travel up the bat handle until one of them gets a thumb over the end. The Waterboro manager wins that contest, so his team gets to bat first and our team takes to the field.

Tonight Jamie is pitching as usual, with Donald catching. I'm on first base, because I am the only one with a first baseman's glove and a hard-earned pair of baseball shoes with steel cleats. Ray Mullett, Joe's older son, is on second, my older brother Art is on third, George Gould is playing short with Fred Gay and Alan and Bobby Mullett are in the outfield.

Everyone on our team has appropriate ball gloves except for Alan Mullett. Alan is left-handed, but he has only a used and misshapen right hander's glove that acts as a cushion for catching the ball. When a ball comes his way, he catches it, takes it out of the glove, then takes off the glove and switches the ball to his left hand so he can throw it and make the play. He is quite adept at this shuffle and often makes a successful play.

We play until it rains, but by that time it's too dark to see the ball, anyway. Everyone gets into their cars and pickup trucks or onto their bicycles and goes home happy to have played a few hours of the all-American game with no clear winners.

# New Year's Day 1953

The traditional highlight of New Year's Day was a come-one-come-all skating party at Round Pond behind the Fish and Game Lodge. This was on the condition of sufficient ice thickness for safe skating. It had been quite cold for a couple of weeks, and an informal committee rendered an opinion that the ice was safe.

Four acres in area, Round Pond is a near-perfect circle; it's mysterious, bottomless and spring-fed with no inlet or outlet, though some think that the outlet may be an underground stream.

At 10 am, after everyone finished morning chores, people were ready for a day of celebration and skating. Piling wood on an old tire and dowsing it with kerosene provided a quick fire, guaranteed to burn, instead of messing around with bits of newspaper, dry kindling and the Boy Scout stuff. We hauled benches and chairs, charcoal grills, picnic lunches and blankets onto the ice near the shoreline.

Soon Dad arrived with his Ford tractor with homemade snow plow blade attached. First, he walked out onto the ice and jumped up and down. Then he nosed the tractor out onto the ice and listened for any cracking sounds. The ice was solid. He then cleared an area about half the size of a football field so folks could play hockey.

Dad began plowing the snow in a large circle around the perimeter of the pond after he had cleared the skating area near the bonfire and the crowd had coffee and burgers. Meanwhile, over in the free-skating area, I was having a minor altercation with an older boy from the other side of town. At the same time I dumped him on the ice by ramming into his skates with a snow scoop, there was a loud crack and a boom across the surface of the ice.

Everyone stopped and peered across the pond to where Dad's tractor had just broken through the ice. Of course, everyone rushed to the scene, but not too close, in case the ice would break under them. By the time I got to where the tractor was, Dad was already clambering up over the hood of the tractor. The stuck plow blade was holding the tractor from going under.

After he made a quick trip home for dry clothes and a warm up, Dad was back and figuring out how to get the tractor out of the pond. Charlie Houston's gravel pit was about a mile away and he had a Caterpillar D6 with a winch. Charlie perched it on a ridge above the back edge of the pond. From there they could run a cable and hook up to the front of the tractor.

While Charlie reeled in his winch, several men broke the ice and guided the tractor up and out of the water onto dry land. They then towed the waterlogged tractor to Ray Burbank's repair garage in the village, leaving an oil slick in its wake.

The skating party continued for a while after the tractor incident, but afternoon chores were calling and soon the crowd packed up and cleared the ice.

Several days later, after the tractor warmed up in the garage and all the ice melted away, Ray drained all the compartments of water-contaminated oil and dried out the electrical components. He cleared the water from the gas tank and the carburetor and soon it was ready for Dad to drive it home.

When Dad started the engine, Ray had left the tractor in gear. The tractor lunged into the garage wall and busted out a hole from which hundreds of empty whiskey bottles tumbled. Dad had no idea Ray was such a drinker.

# Centennial Celebration, 1954

It was seven years after the Great Fire of 1947, and everywhere there was evidence of the destruction that had taken place. Blackened fingers of trees pointed to the sky amid fresh growth bursting with color. Black-eyed Susans and pink and red wild roses that had been long stunted into submission by forest overgrowth now came to life, dressed in blossoms and filling the air with their intoxicating scent. Brooks were again flowing clear and cold, and fish were jumping in the ponds all across the town. Fields had returned to green, cows were grazing and crops were growing. Survival trees were freshly dressed in their many shades of green. Destroyed houses and barns had been replaced with new construction, painted white with fire-resistant asphalt roofs. Some farms had new tractors in fresh, bright colors.

It was a town of mostly farm people and factory workers. With no village commons of its own, the town center was the newly constructed Dayton Consolidated School, situated at the intersection of Routes 5 and 35. As the Fourth of July approached, the atmosphere in town exploded with enthusiasm and anticipation. This was Dayton's centennial, and the celebration aimed to include every one of the five- or six-hundred residents.

There was a pancake breakfast followed by historical skits played on the new school auditorium stage, and a gigantic chicken barbecue for the noontime crowd. There was ice cream and cotton candy, bottles of orangeade, chocolate milk on ice and hot dogs and hamburgers. The carnival-like atmosphere and the aroma of barbecued burgers and hot dogs were nearly overpowering to us youngsters in the crowd.

The Centennial Parade was the largest ever in Dayton. Floats on farm trucks and horse-drawn wagons stretched out for over a half-mile. One float, drawn by a team of oxen, showcased period-costumed ladies on their spinning wheels and looms. One float held the Thornton Academy band ensemble with every schoolboy's dream date — seventeen-year-old Barbara, who wore white buck shoes and played the drums dressed in a maroon uniform decorated with brass buttons and gold braid. One of the parading antique cars made a lasting impression by overheating and shooting a great plume of steam into the air.

I was thirteen on that day as I pondered the meaning of the word, *centennial*. I realized this event wouldn't happen again in my lifetime. Although the festivities ended around four o'clock, when almost every celebrant had to return home to tend to their cows or other farm chores, I have kept that day vivid and alive in my memory.

# A Real Cow Dog

There had been several cow dogs on our farm. The first that I remember was King, a mixed-breed, tawny-colored dog. He was a nice enough dog, but couldn't quite make it in the herding department. King belonged to my brother Art, and I remember how hard he took it when King got under the wheels of a car that was passing by the farm. Next there was Skippy, an English shepherd, mostly. Another nice dog, but Skippy was not really dependable for herding cows, preferring to spend most of her time chasing squirrels in the ample woods around the farm.

One of my jobs at fourteen was to round up all the milk cows and get them into the barn for milking. This was not a simple job, because at 4:30 in the morning the herd would be scattered over a couple of acres and it wasn't quite light out. Rounding up thirty-five cows, herding them through the gate at the top of the hill and pushing them toward and into the barn was difficult and sometimes maddeningly frustrating.

Our tie-up was on the main floor level and the cows had to climb a steep gravel slope into the barn. The certain knowledge of a bucket of grain waiting for them once they were in their stall provided inducement for some, but not all the cows.

By then, Skippy had retired and was no longer with us. It was time for a new dog. This would be *my* dog. A breeder in New Hampshire had an excellent reputation with Border collies, so Dad and Mom drove over one day and brought back a twelve-week-old female. I named her Suzy and soon I began training her.

Ranging back and forth behind the cows with Suzy on a long lead got her used to the herd and got the cows used to her. She had an instinct to herd, and soon Suzy was off the lead and ranging by herself. Over that summer, she turned into a competent cow dog and I thought I was a pretty good dog trainer. Looking back through the lens of time, I have come to understand this young animal had a combination of instinct and intelligence that went far beyond any training I could impart. Soon I didn't even need to go into the field with her. I would stand beside the gate and say, "Go get 'em, Suzy!" and she would soon have the entire herd gathered up and moving through the gate into the barnyard.

Suzy continued to improve throughout that first summer and into the fall when it got cold at night and we confined the cows to the barn full-time. It was a pleasure to watch the way Suzy dominated the herd. As soon as she appeared in the pasture, the cows would become attentive and move toward the barn. If one of them went in another direction, Suzy would head her off and then, coming from behind, she would slip up close and nip the cow on the heel. Sometimes the nipped cow would kick back but Suzy never got hit as she would put her nose to the ground so when the kick came, the hoof would pass just above her ears with no contact.

By the second summer, it was hard to know who was training whom. When the milking herd was in the barnyard beside the barn waiting to go up the ramp into the tie-up, I would go inside and when I came to the window and say, "OK, Suzy!" she would cut out five or six cows and push them up the ramp into the barn. Then she would hold the rest of the herd in place until I came back to the window after closing the stanchions on the six that had come into the tie-up. Again I would say, "Ok Suzy!" and she would deliver another five or six up the ramp. We would repeat this until all thirty-five cows were in the barn and secured in their stalls.

On the rare occasion when Suzy couldn't join me to bring in the herd, I soon learned that without her, the cows didn't want to move at all. So I tried a different tactic. I would pretend she was there and give the imaginary Suzy the same voice commands. Hearing those commands, the cows would react as if she was on the job. Maybe I had trained Suzy, but she had trained the cows.

# Gone Fishin'

Three spring-fed brooks flow year-round across parts of Harris Farm. Two of them originate on the farm, one of which springs fully formed out of a hillside, with clear water so cold it will make your teeth ache when you take a drink.

There are also two man-made irrigation ponds in the large meadow where the best cornfields are located. We three boys and some local youngsters all taught ourselves to swim in those ponds. We had great fun splashing around, cannon-balling and swimming on those hot days of summer. When Mary from down the road or our girl cousins Sandra and Margie were there, it was great fun to swim underwater, grab an ankle and listen for their muffled screams.

The irrigation ponds lacked fish because they were not connected to the nearby flowing brooks. I was about thirteen when I decided it was up to me to correct that deficiency. Gathering up my equipment — a three-gallon pail, a dip net, and a couple of tin cans — I set out for the nearest brook about two hundred yards from the pond. It was already three thirty in the afternoon when I began this activity.

Catching baby trout from a brook and transferring them into a pail of water is not as easy as you might imagine. Intent on my self-imposed task, I lost track of the time; by the time I had made a couple of trips with about a dozen small trout, two hours had already passed.

I should have been in the barn milking the cows by 4:30 at the latest. I came straggling into the farmyard a little after 5:30.

54

"Where have you been and what in tarnation have you been up to? (Dad never used profanity.) We've been calling for you and even blew the horn on the big truck." The ton-and-a-half Ford truck had the loudest horn on the farm and we used it whenever we needed to get someone's attention.

I must have been concentrating really hard to not have heard that.

Dad was very strict about the milking schedule — 4:30 in the morning and 4:30 in the afternoon, allowing a full twelve hours between milkings. He also believed in punishment for disobeying instructions. The punishment for this misdemeanor was for me to cut a switch from the forsythia bush beside the house, and he would administer a few lashes.

I cut a shoot about three feet long, and thick enough to hurt. After stripping off its leaves and small twig branches, I handed it to him. Several lashes across my shirt-covered back and backside and the punishment was over and done. I didn't cry during this punishment and never had to cut another switch.

Today, we frown upon corporal punishment, but if I had a choice, I would always choose a whipping over a "talking to" by Dad. I'm sure he was trying to be a good father and parent, but he did not have the best role model for the job.

Dad was a caring grandfather to our children. Somewhere in the family album I have a Polaroid I took when our kids Carolyn and Richard were little. They crouch in the rich green clover, intent on their grandfather worming a hook so they can catch trout from the pond I had stocked so many years before.

# Lakeside Youth Camp, 1954

I was thirteen years old, and it was my turn to have two weeks with no farm chores at Lakeside Youth Camp in Oakland, Maine. My older brother Art had his camp experience the year before.

I filled the days before camp with preparation. I packed six dazzling white JCPenney tee shirts, three shorts, two pairs of long pants (one green, one blue), six pairs of new socks, sneakers (red), two hats (who needs more than one hat?), three long-sleeved shirts, six white handkerchiefs, swim trunks, two leather belts (really, two?), a wallet with spending money, and a jackknife. Mom sewed labels neatly lettered with India ink onto all my clothes. I would also need soap, toothbrush, and toothpaste in a little bag. Plus a couple of washcloths and towels.

On that Sunday in late August, my cousin Elizabeth drove me and some of our church youth group to the campground. We arrived when it was just getting dark, after having stopped on the way for a meal at the Deering restaurant in Lewiston.

We spent some time at registration and were soon on our way to our assigned cabins. I didn't know anyone in my cabin, as the goal was to make new friends while at camp. They assigned me a bunk and everyone else was already in bed; I hurried and got into my bunk and went quickly to sleep.

Very late that first night, a distant rumble startled me awake. It got louder and louder, and soon all my surroundings were shaking. Was it an earthquake? An airplane crash nearby? It got louder until it became a steady roar that seemed to last forever. Gradually it faded into the distance until it was quiet again.

I awoke the next morning in this strange place, in my strange bed, sharing a cabin with strangers. I didn't know if I had experienced something real or if it was a nightmare. We were told to make our beds, get cleaned up for breakfast and to make our way to the dining hall. As soon as I left the cabin, I got my answer. There, not ten feet from our cabin in the woods, was a railroad track. I hadn't noticed it in the night's dark and confusion.

The camp counselors filled the next two weeks with activities. There were crafts, archery, baseball, nature walks, swimming in Lake Messalonskee, Bible classes, singing, and a few field trips. Each night there was a religious service with altar calls and young people getting saved. I didn't much care for the altar calls, as they made me uncomfortable. I enjoyed the music, especially the Tabor brothers who inspired me to take up the trumpet.

Charlie Brown wasn't the only boy captivated and smitten by a cute girl with curly red hair. And I wasn't the only boy who noticed the red-haired girl. Several of the guys tried to catch her eye, but she chose me to be her friend. Her name was Janice, and she was from Dorchester, Massachusetts and a proper young lady. I, on the other hand, was a very uncultured farm boy. She wasn't bossy, but she quietly and gently influenced me in the rules of courtesy and manners. I think maybe she saw something in me I had no idea was there.

Over the remainder of our camp days, we became good friends and even advanced to the handholding stage. We contrived to sit together during activities and even had a date of sorts when we all went to get treats at an ice cream parlor in Waterville. I put on my best long pants and shirt and she wore a white party dress printed with tiny white flowers. We sat together on the bus and I put my arm around her while she put her head on my shoulder.

The last days of camp were bittersweet. We made promises to write every week, and perhaps the following year we would pick up where we left off. When everyone had left for home and had said their goodbyes, I remember feeling like Charlie Brown, waving goodbye to a little red-haired girl who I would never see again.

# Labor Day, 1954

By ten o'clock in the morning on Labor Day, every able-bodied member of the Goodwins Mills Advent Christian Church was at or on their way to the Ferry Beach Association Campground and a day at the beach. For most of the churchgoers, this was their only day at the beach for the entire year, after a long, hot summer of hard work.

We were riding in our new to us, three-year-old 1951 Ford Custom four-door metallic golden brown sedan with V8 engine and automatic transmission. All the windows were down, with Mom and Dad in front, us three boys in back and a trunk filled to bursting with beach chairs and picnic baskets bulging with sandwiches, salads, iced juices, and cookies.

In a plastic container sat Mom's angel food cake, browned on top and jeweled with tiny globes of sugar, baked to perfection in our cast-iron stove.

Once on Ferry Road, our boyish expectations for the day's promise of a communal picnic, touch football, sand, surf, seaweed, shells and sand dollars were almost too much to bear.

About a half-mile from the beach came the first impact of ocean and salt air. The smell of sand and sun-baked seaweed, the hot sweet fern that lined the trail to the beach, and the bromides that wafted from the surf assaulted our farm-dulled senses.

Already barefoot and in our swim trunks, we jumped from the back seat and bolted for the beach the instant the car came to a halt in the small parking lot beside Seaside Avenue.

"Where do you boys think you are going?" Dad's voice. "Help your mother with the baskets before you go running off." Always some chore to do to take the edge off the fun we were expecting.

After transferring the contents of our car to our picnic table, we covered the 300 yards to the water in a flash. Soon we felt the sand between our toes as we splashed up to our waists in salt surf, daring one another to be the first to duck under the surface.

For a while we ran in and out of the waves with our buddies and strolled down the beach, scuffling through the seaweed looking for treasures and discussing matters of world importance such as what will the new teacher be like or what is the likelihood of getting to sit next to a favorite girl in the classroom.

At the stroke of noon, everyone on the beach returned to the campground and the picnic. We waited for Reverend Osborne to finish his blessing (he seemed to cover a lot of ground in his blessings) and then, thank God, it was time to eat.

As usual, Mom had packed our basket with four kinds of sandwiches plus her signature potato salad. We had thick slices of home-cured ham with cheese and oozing mustard on oversize Cushman white bread, sandwiches stuffed with tuna, egg salad and of course peanut butter with homemade strawberry jam. Let's not forget the three varieties of homemade pickles.

Running in and out of the surf and up and down the beach creates a powerful appetite in growing bodies. Soon all the tables were bare and people were walking around and visiting. Everyone had bits and pieces of dessert to share along with gossip and farm talk.

Soon we moved the tables to the side of the field and the annual touch football game was underway. We formed two equal teams with participants ranging from thirteen to sixty-something. After about forty-five minutes of football, played with no referee, flexible rules and abstract scoring, they declared a winner and everyone but the die-hard footballers returned to the beach. After all, the mandatory half-hour rule had expired, and Mom and Dad could allow us to go swimming again.

The older generation formed a line of beach chairs and sunshades along the white sand, and the gossiping and farm talk continued. Some formed groups to debate religion or politics, while others simply observed the children and teens take turns showing off.

As the afternoon wore on, a cloud that had been hanging on the horizon was getting closer — the knowledge that both this day and summer are coming to a close. At 4:00 we would have to return to the farm to bring in the last load of silage corn, pick sweet corn for the market the next day, gather the cows into the barn for the milking, followed by a quick supper and bed.

We are up early the next morning and after chores, it's off to the first day of school with a unique mixture of dread, enthusiasm and anticipation.

# Lakeside Youth Camp, Revisited

It was the summer of 1956, my seventeen-year-old brother Art and I had finished farm chores and by 7:00 we were on our way to Lakeside Campground on Lake Messalonskee, near Augusta, Maine. It was a fine late August day, warm with blue skies and puffy clouds. As he drove, we talked about how good it was to have the rest of the day off from farm chores.

We had blown the engine in my 1948 Ford coupe on a similar trip the Sunday before so we had to drive the family car, a 1951 Ford four-door sedan, which was in much better condition.

Our parents believed we were driving to Lakeside Youth Camp to experience youth fellowship and to take in the sermons and several religious services. In reality, we were driving the ninety miles to meet up with two female camp counselors, one of whom Art had met at his two-week youth camp experience the previous year and her friend, whom I'd met the week before.

Soon we arrived at the campground and found the two girls. We all dutifully attended the morning service, then skipped out in favor of more personal experiences. Both girls were camp counselors that year and had more liberty than the campers.

We drove around the area and did some sightseeing, had lunch at a diner and found a spot overlooking the lake to watch the "submarine races." Later in the afternoon we returned the girls to the campground, and we all attended the evening service.

After our goodbyes, it was my turn to drive home. Twenty miles of back road driving took us to Augusta where we picked up the

Maine Turnpike south. We planned to drive as far as Lewiston, where we would stop for coffee at the Howard Johnson's before continuing toward home.

As the sun went down and the night air cooled, we rolled up the car windows and turned on a little heat. It had been a long day and fatigue was setting in. Soon Art stopped talking and when I looked over at him, I could see he had fallen asleep. Turnpike driving is quite easy but very boring, especially with no conversation. Listening to music on the radio doesn't help either.

Before I realized it, I was passing the rest stop and the next thing I remember is Art yelling at me to wake up. The car was in the ditch beside the Turnpike, traveling about fifty miles an hour, and we were approaching the abutment of an overpass. This overpass construction included an opening behind the vertical abutment that was next to the highway.

Still moving at forty miles an hour, the car went up on its side and shot through the opening. After about two-hundred feet further along the ditch, we finally came to rest in a cloud of dust. Art had a scratch on his left knee from the radio knob, but I was completely uninjured. We sat for a minute and collected ourselves. Then we started walking back to Howard Johnson's.

The restaurant was open but empty except for a state trooper we'd later come to know as Mageson, who was sitting at the counter with a cup of coffee. He listened to our story and drove us to the scene where, after observing the tire tracks, he shook his head in disbelief. "You boys better be saying your prayers tonight."

When we got back to the rest stop, we called Mom and Dad and Mageson arranged for them to pick us up at the Auburn toll booth. They arrived an hour later in the farm pickup truck. There was only room for three in the truck's cab and they put me in the cab. They relegated Art to the back of the truck for the long drive home.

I was back to driving the next day.

# Touchstone

*Touchstone: 1. A piece of fine grained dark schist or Jasper formerly used for testing alloys of gold by observing the mark that they make on it.
2. A standard or criterion by which something is judged or recognized. Synonyms: criterion, standard, benchmark, yardstick, barometer, bellwether, litmus test.*

It was stifling hot in the packed and tiny country church on that late August evening. The church was hosting its last night of a week-long series of revival meetings. They encouraged everyone to bring a visitor and listen to the evangelist preach about tithing.

It was a Saturday evening and most of the people in the congregation were farmers. Some had probably stopped off at the river or a farm pond for a little wash-up before the service, but quite a few had taken a lick and a promise after working in the field all day before milking the cows and cleaning up the barn. The air, even with all the windows open, was a little thick.

Ma and Pa Cole were in their usual seats, second row on the far right with their family situated close by. Ma, or Edith, was the matriarch of the congregation and the one who most everyone regarded as a healer. She was the one who folks went to in the event of injury or illness. Ma would either fix you up with some sort of remedy or tell you or your parents that a visit to a proper doctor was necessary. It's hard to remember if she was a large woman or if she just had a large presence.

Pa, or Harris, her husband, was short and stocky, a hard worker, always busy and very stooped, and now in his late seventies walked with a limp. Both were colorlessly dressed as usual. The rest of the congregation was mixed. Most were farmers and their families. Some were factory workers in nearby Sanford or Biddeford. All were hard-working folk, and all but a few were members of our church. There may have been a few Baptists or Methodists there, but mostly the three Protestant churches kept separate, except for Sunday evening services, which rotated between the three churches — Advent Christian, Methodist, and Baptist.

The Cole family made up half of the twelve-piece orchestra: Richard on the saxophone, his wife Lois on the French horn, Robert on the banjo, Clark on trombone, Wallace on trumpet and Dorothy on the cello. Doris Smith also played cello and Virginia Gay was on mandolin. Mom and her sister Eleanor were on the violin and Gladys Waterhouse played piano. A fellow called Pierce whose last name I've forgotten played the clarinet. All were members of our church.

Once the music part of the service was over, everyone in the orchestra and the choir usually went to sit in the congregation. On this night with the packed church, the orchestra and the choir stayed in their folding chairs, listening uncomfortably to the evening's sermon.

The evangelist for this series of services was a pretty well-known publisher of Christian publications. His topic for the evening was stewardship. Losing no time getting to the premise of his sermon, he told us that in order to be responsible Christians, we should not only tithe but we also had a responsibility to give it all to the church, keeping only enough to live on. If we could live on twenty dollars per week and were making sixty dollars, we owed the church forty dollars. He went on in this vein for an hour before bringing the service to a close. He was from the big city but was preaching to a congregation of poor farmers who were just getting by scratching a living out of a few acres of crops and milking fifteen or twenty cows.

After the altar call and the benediction, the congregation filed out while the reverend stood on the stoop and shook hands with the exiting folk. I was sixteen and remember observing him.

He wore a hundred-dollar Panama suit, a fifteen-dollar necktie, fifty-dollar shoes, and a frilly silk dress shirt. I wore a wool hand-me-down fifteen-dollar JCPenney suit. When he walked across the lawn onto the gravel parking lot, he slid into his pink and cream 1956 Lincoln Capri coupe and drove regally away to his lakeside vacation home in New Hampshire.

That sound you just heard was my sixteen-year-old touchstone breaking into bits on the anvil of my righteous indignation.

# End of Act II

Down comes the curtain on summer and with a change of props the fall scene begins.

Without warning, the mornings are cooler and the grass wet with heavy dew as we gather the cows for milking. We pick and sell the last of the sweet corn and ready the standing stalks for grinding into silage that we will store in the tall silo at the back of the barn.

School has started and Dad works alone until we boys get home at about three o'clock. Days are suddenly shorter, and there is a sense of urgency in the air. Fall is a time for putting things away before the approaching winter. There are forty-five acres of standing corn to cut, chop and load into the silo where we will tread it down until we work out all the air to retard spoilage.

There is the fall harrowing of the cornfields, followed by sowing of winter wheat and rye to stabilize and energize the soil for spring plowing. We bring in wood from the woodlots and saw and stack it in the shed where it will be dry and ready for winter heating.

There is equipment to clean and store in the equipment shed, and a third crop of hay full of alfalfa and clover to mow. The bales are heavy with milk-producing nutrients.

So little time and so much to do until the final curtain signals the beginning of winter.

# air

# Sammy

His name was Samuel, but everyone called him Sammy. He was tall and painfully thin and walked with an ambling gait, leaning forward with his head down. He wore flannel shirts and bib overalls that he was constantly outgrowing. He wasn't bad, just different. Some would say he was slow. Others would say he couldn't cope with school.

His mother, Grace, was a single mom whose husband had died early. Sammy was her oldest son. His younger brother Mike enjoyed school and was active at the local church youth group. They lived in an old white farmhouse with a barn in need of paint and some acreage about a mile out of town across the Mills Road from the slaughterhouse.

Grace worked full-time seven miles away at the county courthouse, so she left the boys on their own to take care of themselves. She felt guilty about it, but it was the only way to keep food on the table and a roof over their heads. Mike had the responsibility of looking out for his older brother Sammy and keeping him out of trouble. They took Sammy out of school by the second grade because the teacher said he couldn't learn.

As the two boys got older and Mike got more involved in school, Sammy had to take care of himself. Unable to read or write, he couldn't pass a driver's exam, so he always either walked or rode his bicycle. He would often walk the mile into the village to hang out at the general store, where the storekeeper's beautiful daughter, Barbara, was in charge of the soda fountain.

The local kids and some adults were mean to Sammy and would tease him about Barbara, or they would talk him into doing things that he shouldn't do, like urinating on an electric fence or throwing rocks at passing cars. Then they would laugh at him and make him cry. Sammy didn't get angry or fight back. He would just hunch up his shoulders, lifting his too short overalls up to the middle of his calves, saunter to his bike and head home.

Sammy was brilliant at taking things apart and repairing them. He built his bicycles from parts he found in the dump or that people gave him. He constructed beautiful scale model airplanes from bits of wood and paper, and then he would take them to the top of the barn and fly them out the window after setting them on fire to watch them crash. I don't recall ever hearing of him hurting anyone or being mean to animals.

Until I went off to college, I remember Sammy as a fixture around the village, fishing in the millpond, hanging around the general store, being teased by the locals and riding his raggedy bike. At twenty-five, Sammy was still living with his mother. By then, Mike had graduated high school and joined the Army.

By the time I had finished school, Sammy's mother had died, and the farm had been sold. Sammy was taken to live in an institution, I don't know where. When I returned to visit, the village seemed a little poorer for his loss.

# Welcome to Fort Dix

On October 4th, 1963, the Selective Service board in Kennebunk, Maine mailed me an Order to Report for Induction on October 22, 1963 at 7:15 am.

I hadn't planned on being drafted into the US Army at age twenty-two. I had just graduated from Maine Vocational Technical Institute where I had studied automotive technology. I thought I had things pretty much in order, with Nancy, who had recently become my fiancée, a new job and a new apartment.

I had very mixed feelings. I was sad to leave my job and all my friends behind. Nancy had returned to college in New Hampshire and I had moved all my things into storage at the family farm. I was angry at the Army for upsetting my plans. When my draft notice came, I was in the last stages of enlisting in the Air National Guard in Cape Elizabeth where I was scheduled to take officer's training and be assigned as a second lieutenant at the motor pool.

The Army Induction Center on Forest Avenue in Portland dealt with all the last-minute details, and after a short bus ride to the Portland Airport, they loaded us into an airplane to Newark Airport. By that point I had come to terms with the situation and I was excited. Excited to be taking a trip in a big multi-engine aircraft, excited to begin basic training and to see just what the Army might find for me to do. I imagined the Army would capitalize on my civilian training and experience in the automotive and heavy equipment maintenance field.

Naive me.

On the 23rd of October, the Army introduced me to my new home — Fort Dix, New Jersey. We spent the next several days at the Army Reception Center where they issued us uniforms, equipment and everything we would need in the way of clothing for basic training.

The first order of business involved getting a military haircut. For me it was not at all traumatic as I kept my thick hair short in a "flat top." Some young men had "greaser" hairdos and I remember the Army barbers taking great delight in cutting their hair up from the back leaving the top and front for the last where they would run the clippers across and all the mass of hair would come off at once. I saw many new recruits with tears in their eyes at the sudden change in appearance.

After the haircuts came a battery of shots for protection against every imaginable disease. The Army administrated these shots by using a needle machine with compressed air injection system. Lined up single file, they guided us along a path between medical personnel. One and sometimes two at a time, we got all our shots and came out at the end with a couple dozen little red marks on our arms and other places.

I stood in line for a blood test, extended my finger so the tech could take a finger prick blood sample, and then continued on to the medical station waiting area. One fellow in line was so terrified that by the time he got to the tech he had turned deathly white and was on the verge of passing out. He made it past the medical station and walked directly into the wall where he passed out cold.

Later on I got to know this young man as a "Sergeant Bilko" type who was always promoting a poker game, especially just after payday. We received our pay in cash once a month. All $77.10 of it.

After the haircuts, shots, uniforms and equipment and intelligence and aptitude testing, we moved into our new home. Company C, Third Training Regiment was located right next to the runway at McGuire Air Force Base and comprised a dusty parade ground surrounded by two-story wooden barracks from the Second World War, painted in faded yellow. The only green that existed was the color of our uniforms.

We quickly were becoming acclimated to training mode. Because of my prior ROTC training at the University of Maine, they assigned me to squad leader, and I wore an armband with the sergeant stripes. That meant I didn't have to do kitchen patrol or guard duty.

There were eight young men in my squad and we quickly melded into a cohesive unit. My duties as squad leader included making sure my men were all present and accounted for at formations, meals and all training sessions. When I say my squad quickly became a cohesive unit, I mean that we looked out for each other. For example, if one man lost an article of his "kit," other members of the squad would "find" the article and return it to him. Meanwhile, a member of some other squad would suddenly notice the absence of this article. Inspections were frequent, and any missing article from the Army-issued training kit was subject to punishment.

Every day was busy from early morning to late afternoon with something different just about every hour. There were lectures in the open while standing at parade rest, interrupted frequently by the overpowering sound of fighter jets taking off one hundred yards away at the Air Force Base. At every break they gave the order: "Smoke 'em if you've got 'em. Field strip the butts." I think almost every Army trainee became a smoker because of this order.

Classes on chemical, biological, and radiological warfare; classes on camouflage; classes on weapon maintenance; manual of arms, parade and drill, ten-mile marches with full battle gear, a mile run in the morning before breakfast, formations and critique. There were classes on hand-to-hand combat and finally night infiltration where we crawled on our bellies through a simulated battle scene with explosions going off in bunkers and barbed wire in every direction.

During the fourth week, we took marksmanship training at the rifle range. On November 22, 1963, after everyone had finished shooting, we all loaded into the trucks and rode back to Charlie Company for formation and dismissal for the weekend. In formation that day, we learned of the assassination of President John F. Kennedy in Texas that afternoon. At first everyone thought the sergeant was making a very cruel joke. The irony of our being on the rifle range shooting military rifles while our president was being assassinated by a man shooting a military rifle didn't immediately occur to us.

As reality settled in, the rumors began. Only a couple years earlier, the Bay of Pigs fiasco had occurred and the Cuban missile crisis of 1962 was still fresh in our memory. The Cold War was at its height, and wild speculations were rampant. First, that we were going to have an abbreviated basic training after which they would ship us to a front in Europe to be ready to retaliate against the Russians, who must have been behind this atrocity. Next, we were to take over Cuba, because Castro must have engineered the assassination. Then it was the Mafia behind it, and the military would round up the villains.

After a long weekend of watching the news on TV in the dayroom, training resumed with time off to observe the presidential funeral. Rumors and speculations were quelled, and things returned to a nervous quiet.

In December it was so cold they canceled our scheduled bivouac at Fort Dix. Training in things like gas attack readiness and physical fitness tests filled our days. The troops were excited about Christmas leave and catching up with family. On December 6th we finished qualifying at the rifle range and things sort of relaxed. I was feeling good, having qualified as an expert with the M1 rifle.

After Christmas we were back to Fort Dix for a last week of training and to wait for our next orders. I received orders to report to the Army Veterinary Food Inspection Service School in Chicago, Illinois, for an eight-week training course to become a Food Inspection Specialist. That, of course, is the beginning of another story.

# AWOL Airways

Dexter Cox was a fellow draftee and new friend from the US Army Veterinary Food Inspection Service school in Chicago. He was also an experienced pilot and owner of a T-50 that he had flown from his home in Casper, Wyoming to attend the school.

After two months of full-time school, we were getting a little restless. It was time for an adventure. We all carried Class A passes with a 150-mile limit and slept in the barracks, so living was cheap. By pooling our resources, we could have some real fun.

Dexter, myself, and our new east coast schoolmates, John and Dennis, hatched a plot one evening. We would leave on Friday afternoon, each with a small bag packed with civilian clothes for the weekend. If anyone asked what our plans were, we would say we were renting a car to tour the nearby sights for the weekend. No big deal.

Directly after class let out, we gathered our things and grabbed a taxi to Midway Airport. After a thorough pre-flight examination of the airplane, Dexter walked the propellers through two complete revolutions to clear any residual oil from the bottom cylinders before climbing in and starting the engines. The airplane was an Army training airplane from the forties and looked identical to the Songbird depicted in the black-and-white TV serial *Sky King*. This plane was to carry us, round-trip, from Chicago to Maine. The weather report promised fair skies for the three days ahead.

Soon we were in the air, navigating towards the East Coast. Chicago's city lights were just blinking on as we climbed over the city, and a magnificent panorama spread out before us. The bright colors of the cars and buildings passed beneath us as we cleared the city soon muted into shades of gray as darkness set in. Once we had reached our cruising altitude of about 5000 feet, individual cars were only pinpricks of light on the highways between the splashes of lights from the towns and cities.

Inside the airplane, we were excited to be on a weekend adventure. In normal flying conditions, the hot air ducted from the engines warms the cabin. However, at 5000 feet in February, dressed in our woolen army uniforms and wrapped up in our wool-lined Army greatcoats, we were still cold. By the time we got to Cleveland, Ohio for a fuel and rest stop, we were ready for a warm terminal building and some hot coffee.

After warming up and filling the fuel tanks with 100 dollars' worth of gasoline and a couple gallons of oil for the engines, we were off and flying towards our next stop — Albany, New York. The atmosphere in the cabin was a little subdued as we contemplated the seriousness of our trip. The sky was very dark on the horizon and with the unpredictability of the weather, and going through a couple minor snow squalls, we realized the way ahead could be dangerous. Adding to this was the fact we were officially AWOL as soon as we passed the 150-mile limit.

When we arrived at Albany at 2:30 in the morning, we were ready for another warm up and coffee. We passengers had probably dozed a little on the flight, but had no restful sleep. Dexter impressed me in that he could stay awake at the controls, navigate in the dark from one city to the next, talk to air traffic control, locate the proper approach to unfamiliar airports and safely land.

We were off again by 3:00 into the darkest part of the night. Now there were mountains between us and the coast, and we had to pick a route to avoid them. As we crossed into Massachusetts, the horizon ahead lightened and soon we could see objects on the ground. When we landed at the New Bedford Airport in the early hours of morning, John and Dennis departed for their homes. We had all agreed to meet at 9:00 Sunday morning for the trip back to Chicago. With any luck, we would be back at the school in the late afternoon.

From New Bedford, I called home and let the folks know we would land at the Portland, Maine airport at about 7:30. When we got to Maine, we detoured and flew low over the farm before continuing to Portland. By the time we had parked the airplane and arranged the overnight tie down, Dad had arrived to take us to the farm. Home at last to one of Mom's big breakfasts and a much-needed nap before continuing on, by car, to New London, New Hampshire to spend the day with Nancy, my fiancée.

My brother Bill lent me his '62 Ford coupe and soon Dexter and I were on the way to New Hampshire. The roads were clear, and the sky was a brilliant bright blue with puffy white clouds. We made good time and arrived at Colby Junior college a little after noon. Nancy and her good friend Linda met us at their dorm and after introductions the girls signed themselves out for the afternoon and evening. Their weekend curfew was 11:00 sharp.

It was a lovely winter afternoon in the mountains of New Hampshire. We had lunch in a local restaurant and toured around some nearby towns, talking, window-shopping and just enjoying each other's company. In Sunapee we visited the resort where the Colby students took ski lessons. Later we found a local diner for dinner.

In the interest of brevity and decorum, I won't go into the primary activities of that evening. We delivered the girls back to their college dormitory in time for curfew, then drove back to the farm. We were finally in bed by 1:30 in the morning.

Four hours later, we shaved, changed into our dark-green US Army uniforms and had a quick breakfast. Dad gave us a ride to the Portland airport and wished us a safe trip back to Chicago. At the FAA office we got a weather briefing, and at the general aviation terminal we paid the airport fees for the overnight airplane parking. The weather prediction was marginal, but it looked as if we had a good chance of missing a storm that was threatening.

After a thorough preflight check, making sure the fuel tanks were full and once again walking the propellers through two full revolutions, Dexter started the engines. It had been bitterly cold during the night, and those engines turned very slowly for several revolutions before finally catching and running. It seemed like forever before the engine temperature came up into the green and some heat made its way into the cabin.

We took off from Portland at about 7:30, setting a course for New Bedford airport in Massachusetts, and by 9:00 we had picked up John and Dennis and received an update on the weather. Next stop: Albany, New York. Dexter was a fully instrument-rated pilot, capable of navigating in blind conditions. His airplane, however, did not have instruments for flying in blind conditions. There were times on our flight from New Bedford to Albany, especially crossing the White Mountains of New Hampshire, that clouds blinded our way for a disturbingly long time. Crossing southern Vermont, we encountered several snow squalls that we passed through and around. We landed at Albany with light snow falling at about 10:30.

Expecting to make a quick stop, gas up the plane, get a quick lunch and a weather update, we parked the plane and headed for the terminal. We were looking forward to returning to Chicago in the late afternoon. But the FAA station gave us some bad news — worsening weather to the west with snow and icing conditions.

Since our airplane did not have the equipment to operate under IFR (Instrument Flight Rules) conditions, we could not get permission to file a flight plan for Chicago. Stranded in Albany, we had three choices: we could wait for the weather to change, hoping that we would still have time to make it to Chicago in time to avoid AWOL, or we could take a train to Chicago, or try to get on a commercial flight.

We talked it over and waited to see what the weather would do. A train was out of the question as we would never get to Chicago in time. All afternoon we waited for the weather to improve. No luck. Finally, at the last possible moment, we got tickets for the last four seats on a commercial flight to Chicago with one stop in Detroit, Michigan. Because we were flying Military Standby, we were in danger of being put off the flight in Detroit if a regular customer wanted our seats. We agreed our best bet was to stay strapped in place when the plane landed in Detroit, so the airline would have to remove us by force if anyone wanted our seats.

After that short layover we were still in our seats and headed to Chicago. We made plans to pool our resources once again so Dexter could fly to Albany the following weekend to retrieve his stranded airplane.

We landed in Chicago at 10:45 pm, and were off the plane and at the taxi stand by 11:00. Jumping into the first available taxi, we asked the driver if he could get us to Chicago's south side, near the stockyards by 11:30, knowing that normally it takes about forty-five minutes for the trip. "Buckle up!" he yelled as we lurched forward and took one too many two-wheeled corners.

At precisely 11:28 we pulled up to the school barracks, paid the taxi fare and breathlessly arrived at the dayroom where the desk sergeant checked us in and asked, "Did you boys have a good weekend?"

# Overpacked Weekend

I took a week's leave from my duties in St. Louis to attend the wedding of my brother Art to Judy Mesler in Buffalo, New York. I, with my one suitcase, met Nancy with her three suitcases in New Jersey, and together we took a bus from Port Authority in New York City to Biddeford, Maine. We would join Mom, Dad and brother Bill for the drive from the farm in Dayton to Buffalo. Dad's Ford Galaxy was full to the gills and Mom had packed a basket lunch for the roadside rest stops.

At one country rest stop in Vermont, the June fields were green and approaching full maturity. Next to the car park there was a sparkling creek with clear water dodging around the rocky bed. We ate our lunch in grateful silence and watched a great blue heron stalk fish in the cold bubbling current.

After a very long and tiring day of driving, we finally arrived in Buffalo and located our hotel for the weekend. Someone from the wedding party met us at the hotel and brought us to a local restaurant for dinner. Back to the hotel, in separate rooms of course, we fell into bed. Nancy and I spent the next day with Judy's energetic Great-aunt Mabel, who was in her eighties and took it upon herself to give us a whirlwind tour.

We explored both sides of Niagara Falls, spent a lot of time in a botanical garden on the Canadian side, and visited the observation tower with the rotating restaurant in the City of Niagara Falls. We returned to Buffalo in time for the rehearsal and then to the rehearsal dinner, where one of the older men in the wedding party approached Dad with, "Hey, you look like a beer drinker. What'll you have?"

"Water." Dad, a lifelong teetotaler, not only didn't drink alcohol, he had no patience with those who did.

We were up early the next day to prepare for the wedding. We had a nervous breakfast with the other men in the wedding party, then went back to the hotel to dress in the day's uniform: white dinner jacket, frilly white shirt with French cuffs, cummerbund, bow tie, black pants with the satin side stripe, and black shoes. Soon we were off to the church to usher the guests: friends and family of the bride on one side and of the groom on the other side. Everything in readiness: enter the bridesmaids, enter the flower girls, enter Judy, radiant on her father's arm.

Finally, the wedding is over, and we're on to the reception and the wedding feast. Another late night that ends with a bon voyage to the newlyweds and a goodbye to my parents and brother Bill, who would return to Maine at the crack of dawn. Nancy and I would catch a flight midmorning from Buffalo to Chicago and transfer to St. Louis, Missouri, where we would elope a couple of months later.

Although we overslept, our taxi arrived in time to catch the flight from Buffalo to Chicago. The connection to St. Louis would be tight with not much of a layover. Back then, when you had a multi-leg flight, you had to retrieve your baggage and re-check it in for your next flight. The terminals at O'Hare airport in Chicago formed a giant U, with the arrivals coming in on the eastern side and the departures on the western side. The distance around that giant U was about a mile. All the baggage came to the bottom of the U.

When we got to O'Hare, we checked the information desk. Our flight to St. Louis would leave in thirty minutes at the gate at the farthest end of the departure terminal. There were no underground tunnels to carry passengers across from one part of the U to the other, and no fast-moving walkways to speed you along. We walked to the bottom of the U where our baggage should be.

We were running out of time and the baggage had not arrived, so I sent Nancy on ahead to find the departure gate and check us in while I waited for the baggage. Finally, with about eight minutes until last boarding call, I had the four suitcases, two under each arm. I ran as fast as I could for the departure gate. Imagine a half-mile run with an awkward, hundred-pound load with loudspeakers announcing, "Mr. Harris, your flight is ready to depart. We will close the cabin doors in five minutes."

I made it to the gate just as they were closing the doors to the walkway leading to the airplane. They held the door and took my baggage. Nancy was waiting for me in the last two seats at the very back of the plane. Exhausted and dripping with perspiration, I slumped into the last seat on the airplane as the crew readied for takeoff. It was not until the flight crew requested us to put our seats in the upright position and fasten our seat belts for landing in St. Louis that I had a normal heart rate and had stopped perspiring.

"Ladies and gentlemen, welcome to St. Louis. We hope you enjoy your stay."

# My First Solo

At a very young age, when asked what they wanted to be when they grew up, my friends would answer: farmer, doctor, nurse, firefighter, police officer or lawyer. But my answer, from as far back as I can remember, was: airplane pilot.

During World War II, Dad had two military deferments. First as a molder in a foundry and later as a farmer with a family to support. However, he and Mom fulfilled their patriotic duty as air raid wardens by making sure everyone on the roads near the farm had all lights out or sufficiently covered at night. The enemy couldn't bomb what they couldn't see.

One of my earliest memories was in late 1944. I woke in the night to the sound of an airplane approaching. The sound terrified me as it got louder and louder. I could only rest again once I heard it going away. I knew that it couldn't drop a bomb on us after it had passed.

Airplanes and flying have always been an obsession. As a very young boy working on the farm, I would run outside any time I heard an airplane and scan the sky until I could see it. If we were working in the fields, hoeing corn or turning hay and an airplane flew over, I stopped working as long as the airplane was in sight.

In the late 1940s and into the 1950s, during the Korean War, there would be trainers from the Air Guard flying practice over our farm. It was thrilling to watch and imagine I was that pilot.

In grade school, I read every book in the school library that had anything to do with flying. There were adventure books about

WW II battles and books about the theory of flight and about how to build airplanes and how to operate airplane controls. By the time I was in seventh grade, I felt sure that if I had a chance, I could just climb into an airplane and fly it as good as anybody.

One day we were working in the barnyard and suddenly out of nowhere a bright yellow Piper Cub appeared. It was flying dangerously low and at the last second pulled up and barely missed the top of our barn. I learned later that the pilot was Dad's brother, Earl. For quite a long time after that, I was in awe of Uncle Earl who had no formal pilot training but learned to fly from one of his friends.

My first airplane ride was at the Old Town Airport near the University of Maine at Orono, where I spent a year at college. Two of my friends and I chartered a half-hour demonstration ride in a Ryan Navion, a four-seater plane, very sleek with a low wing. I was thrilled to be on an airplane and learned that the motion of flying was totally enjoyable.

Stationed in St. Louis, Missouri after Nancy and I had eloped, I decided it was time for flying lessons.

About ten miles out of St. Louis, we came across a little grass-strip airport that advertised flying lessons and banner towing. Soon we were talking with Dale, the instructor pilot. He offered me a free demonstration ride and in no time signed me up for lessons. Over the next several months and after about twelve hours of instruction, it was time to qualify to solo the little yellow Piper Cub in which I had been training.

To do a proper first solo, the student lets off the instructor who stays on the ground to observe and (I imagine) grow a few gray hairs worrying about crashes. The student pilot then taxis to the end of the field and goes through a checklist and begins the takeoff run. It requires three takeoffs and three landings to a full stop to qualify to solo. The full stop requirement means the student has to turn the airplane around and taxi back to the apron again, another turn around and get ready for another takeoff.

On my second turn around I slightly missed the taxiway. It had rained earlier and one of the landing wheels sank into the mud. I tried to coax the wheel out by applying some power and wiggling the tail. Finally, I had to get out and lift the wheel from the mud with no help from the instructor as solo means you're on your own. Out of the mud and one more takeoff and landing later, my instructor was signing me off as a solo pilot.

If there is a bigger rush and a bigger sense of accomplishment than that first solo in an airplane, I don't know what it might be. Maybe getting married or seeing your first child, but soloing an airplane is right up there. There is an affirmation and a boost to self-confidence that carries over into everyday life, a feeling that if you can solo an airplane, anything is possible.

# Unlimited Visibility

Depending on the weather, we could either fly our 1941 Taylorcraft airplane from the airport in Houlton, Maine, or drive six hours by automobile to attend the wedding of an old friend at the Goodwins Mills Advent Christian Church. Saturday morning dawned bright and clear with unlimited visibility for the weekend. With the good weather prediction, the adventure of flying to and landing on the family farm won out.

We finished our preflight inspection at about 7:00 and with a full tank of gasoline and one suitcase to share (an extra suitcase would have overloaded the craft) we lifted off and took a heading southbound to our first waypoint, Pittsfield, twenty miles west of Bangor. With my co-pilot Nancy keeping track of the chart and picking out landmarks, we had no trouble locating the airport at Pittsfield and dropped in for a fresh tank of gasoline and a bathroom break.

Soon we were off again and following Interstate 95 South to Saco was uncomplicated and at 2500 foot altitude we enjoyed the sights — dollhouse-sized towns with dark-blue ribbons of rivers and creeks and the silver-blue mirrors of lakes and ponds. Off to the west, we could see Mt. Washington and the surrounding ranges. The fields of corn rippled in the breezes with their yellow tassels against the green, and the hayfields were a rich green just coming into the second crop of hay.

As we approached Saco and Biddeford, we banked west and picked out Route 5 to follow across the Saco River into Dayton, the location of the family farm.

Approaching at about 400 feet, we circled the farm twice to determine wind direction and to inspect an open grass-covered field. Satisfied with our landing inspection, we climbed back to 1000 feet and made a standard left-hand pattern approach to a short field landing: *downwind to a point approximately even with the intended landing spot; close the throttle and apply carburetor heat; drop altitude to about 400 feet; turn left in a glide while losing altitude; then take another left turn onto final approach; be mindful to keep the airspeed comfortably above the stall speed.* Nancy kept a close eye on the airspeed to let me know if we were getting close to stall.

We cleared the trees and utility wires at the end of the field using the "forward sideslip approach" and got our wheels on the ground quick enough to avoid overrunning the field at the other end. A safe, successful landing.

Later in the afternoon, when the wedding and festivities were over and the newlyweds had departed on their honeymoon, I flew the airplane to the Sanford Airport for a fresh tank of gasoline to prepare for our early Sunday departure. The takeoff in the cool of the late afternoon was quick and easy with a half tank of gas, no passengers and no suitcase. The landing on return was easy, with favorable winds that enabled me to approach without worrying about the trees and utility wires. I tied down the airplane for the night between two of the trees at the east end of the field.

With the breeze from the west, it seemed like the best takeoff would be to the west.

By the time we were ready to leave on Sunday morning, the sun was high and the day was getting hot. We said goodbye to family, propped the engine and climbed into the cockpit. I noticed Bill had his movie camera with him but didn't give it much thought. We had a full tank of gas, pilot and copilot and a suitcase on board, and the wind was fluctuating. Common sense and good judgment might have been to delay for better conditions, but we did not want to arrive in Houlton in the dark. Our airplane had no electrics and was not legal for flying at night.

I applied the brakes and advanced the throttle for a full run-up. Warmed up and performing at maximum, we released the brakes and began the takeoff run. I picked out a spot on the field where we had to be in the air if we were to clear the trees at the end of the field. With the grass slowing us down we didn't pick up much speed and by the time we got to the spot we were not yet airborne. I put the tail down by pulling back on the controls and the wheels cleared. It was too late to turn back.

If we pulled the nose of the airplane any higher as we approached the trees and the utility wires we could stall and crash; if we continued to gradually climb, we may not clear the trees and wires. What happened next was nothing short of a miracle. A gust of wind lifted us just enough. We cleared by a matter of one or two feet and climbed into the free air above the farm. We caught our breath as we circled once more and navigated north towards home.

Later, Bill gave me his film footage of that takeoff so I could see for myself how frightening it was to witness. From the comfort of my easy chair I watched how the plane disappeared into the forest's pointed teeth but came clear through to the other side, unscathed and unharmed. Blessed by the One With Unlimited Visibility.

# New Jersey Christmas, 1969

Adulthood is about making practical choices. We'd exchanged our Taylorcraft for a washer-dryer set after our daughter Carolyn was born. Now we had another choice: a long drive or short commercial flight to New Jersey to celebrate Christmas with Nancy's parents. After weighing our options, we decided it would be a lot quicker to fly and they'd have more time with their newest granddaughter. We'd just sit back and relax on Presque Isle's Yellowbird to Boston, then transfer to a United Airways flight to Newark. What could go wrong?

December 23rd dawned clear with high clouds and impending storms in the forecast. We were up early, traveling as light as you can with a ten-month-old baby. At Presque Isle Airport, we were checked in almost immediately, and soon we were seated in the big yellow airplane and in the air by 9:00.

Carolyn was a little cranky as we gained height, but settled into a nap soon after we got to cruising altitude. In Boston we picked up our luggage and found our way to the United Airlines departure gate. While we waited for the flight to Newark, we listened to the weather forecasts predicting stormy weather over the next few days.

It was mid-afternoon by the time we had landed at Newark and were riding in a big Pontiac sedan, with Nancy's dad at the wheel. It was getting dark by the time we pulled in to their L-shaped ranch on Lawrence Avenue in an upper-middle-class neighborhood. Christmas decorations were everywhere and multi-colored lights sparkled and reflected in the light snow that was falling.

After dinner, we got Carolyn to sleep early in her crib in the guest room. Exhausted from our trip, we quickly called it a day and trundled off to bed ourselves.

We had a busy day planned for Christmas Eve, so we were up early the next morning. Grandma Helen babysat so Nancy could show me around town in Helen's Dodge Lancer. We visited several of her childhood friends and had lunch at a Woolworth's lunch counter. Thick snow fell as we attended Christmas Eve service at the Westfield Methodist Church and later enjoyed cocktails at home with the grandparents.

Of course, Carolyn was too young to appreciate Christmas, but she had a good time with the wrapping paper. By the time Christmas dinner was over, we were watching the weather and calling the airlines to confirm our return reservations. It had snowed heavily Christmas Eve and was still coming down steadily. Newark Airport was closed and might re-open by the 28th, the day of our return flight.

We spent our next days reading the weather reports and phoning the airlines hourly to see if we could return to Houlton in time on Sunday to be back on the job by Monday. Finally, an operator from United had the answer we wanted — they would be back in operation for our Sunday morning flight to Boston.

When we got to Newark to check in for our flight, we found three days' worth of passengers waiting to board in the overcrowded lounge. The airline representative said they would put on a couple of extra airplanes and they would accommodate everyone. We gave Carolyn to Grandma Helen while we checked our luggage to Boston and waited near the boarding desk at the edge of the milling crowd of anxious passengers when they called out our names to board.

There was no time and no way to push through the unbudging crowd. When the airline representative yelled, "You have to get on now or let someone else have your place!" we motioned to the grandparents that they'd have to pass Carolyn over the heads of the crowd. First Carolyn was passed to a hesitant lady at the edge of the crowd who passed her to another and to another, and so on until she arrived in the arms of a much-relieved Nancy. Even an antagonistic crowd cannot resist the charm of a baby.

After shouting our thanks and goodbyes, we made it onto the waiting airplane. We sat in a row of seats directly in line with the propellers of a Lockheed Electra G, infamously known for crashes due to failed engine mounts. Although I knew this airplane had received the updated engine mounts, I watched them all the way to Boston.

When we got to Boston, we missed our connection to Presque Isle, so after a few tense moments and some discussion, the airline booked us into a local hotel for the night and arranged transportation to get there.

The bellboy showed us to our room and said someone would be along with a baby crib in a few minutes and that the dining room was open for room service if we were interested. We opted for room service since it was well past 7:00, and we were tired and hungry.

While waiting for the crib, we put Carolyn on the bed with a pillow on each side and tried to get her to sleep. We probably dozed off. Suddenly, a bump and a wail. Carolyn had rolled off the bed and thumped her head on the nightstand on her way to the heavily carpeted floor. She was more scared than hurt but now we had an unhappy baby, no crib and still no meal and it was 9:00. Another call to the front desk produced the crib, and we could put Carolyn safely to bed.

At about 10:00 our meal came. So by 11:30 our room contained one sleeping baby and two sleeping adults.

The next morning I called my office to report I would not be back in Houlton until Tuesday because of storm delays. After a complimentary breakfast and a taxi ride back to the airport, we checked in for the flight to Presque Isle. Once on board the Yellow Bird and in the air, the pilot announced the ride would be bumpy and we had to stay buckled up. However, the runways were clear at destination and we should arrive on schedule.

When we got to Presque Isle, the runways were clear, but there was a severe cross-wind. As we approached the landing, I could see we were crabbing into the wind at about thirty degrees to counter the crosswind. The airplane gave a severe lurch as it righted itself and stayed on the runway to complete the landing. On the ground, safe and sound.

Perhaps it might have been easier to drive.

# water

# An Awakening

*"Put those cucumber seeds five to a hill and cover them with a quarter inch of soil. Here, let me show you..."*

And so it went on our very large family garden in one of my earliest memories. Every year we planted and harvested enough vegetables and root crops to carry our family of five for the year — canned, frozen, pickled and stored in the root cellar of our little house. In the forties and fifties, we also planted eight acres of potatoes for market and home use. Our major crop was corn, about thirty acres of sweet corn for the market and thirty acres of silage corn to fill the silo and feed to the cows to supplement the hay and grain.

Summers were long, hot and dry and sometimes dark and rainy, but always with work to do in the cornfields, the gardens and the hayfields. Before my two brothers and I were ten, we were experts in planting, weeding, hoeing, turning and shaking the newly mown hay to make it dry faster, and side dressing the corn with nitrogen granules to make it grow faster and produce bigger ears.

We hoed, weeded, irrigated, picked the corn and potatoes, mowed the hay, raked the hay, baled it and stored it away in the barn, milked the cows and did the barn chores and fell into bed after dark. Sundays we went to church and rested, only doing the milking and the barn chores.

In 1965, when I was twenty-four years old and married, Nancy and I bought our first house in South Portland. There was a backyard big enough for a small garden, and I set out with great confidence. I borrowed my brother Bill's tiller and tilled up an area about twenty by forty feet and then stopped cold with the realization I had no experience in the planning of a garden. I had always been told the where and how. As a result, I knew everything about gardening and I knew nothing about gardening.

# The Great Oak

I was four years old when my family moved to what we would later know as Harris Farm in Dayton, Maine. George, the oak tree, already over one-hundred years old, greeted us as trees do — with a whisper only the young-at-heart can hear.

After we had settled in, Dad installed two swings on George's long horizontal branch. Each swing was a thick pine board that had  notches in each end for the calf chains Dad looped up and over the branch. They wouldn't pass the safety standards of today, and when you really got up to speed, you could swing perilously over the driveway about twenty feet above the ground.

I like to visit George, who still stands tall at the corner of the lower driveway. The swing branch is still there and looks solid. I bet you could still get a pretty good swing going. Though, at my age, I'm not sure I would have the courage to pump up to a twenty-foot height.

George doesn't talk much, but he has always been a good listener. If George is as old as I think he is, then he may have heard people talk about President Lincoln's Gettysburg Address and maybe listened in while they discussed the Lincoln and Douglas debates. I'm sure he probably even saw some Buzzells and Clarks and maybe even one of the Cole boys ride by on the road heading to Biddeford and onwards to the Civil War.

When George was a sapling, rail lines were being built and trains were steaming all over the place carrying passengers and freight. Until he was in his fifties, the only transportation George saw on the two-track Buzzell Road were saddle horses, oxcarts and horse-drawn wagons.

Think of it. In George's lifetime, 99.9 percent of all modern technological advancement on this planet has happened — the invention of electricity, the telephone, automobile, airplane, television, and the rise of computers, nuclear power and mobile phones. Men have landed on the moon, space stations circle the earth, the internet is everywhere with artificial intelligence monitoring our every move — and all this time, George continues to grow, stand guard, ready to listen to anyone. Nobody swings from his branch now, but I think it would be good to re-instate the swing, watch, wait and see what happens.

# Special Delivery

Outside the farmhouse, light snow was falling in the bitter cold. Inside the farmhouse, it was warm as our family waited to ring in the New Year.

It was unusual that we three brothers were together this evening. Bill and Dixie along with their boys were now operating Harris Farm. Art, Judy and their three boys had traveled from upstate New York and were staying on the farm for the Christmas and New Year holidays. Nancy and I had driven down from South Portland with our two kids to join in the fun. There must have been eleven or twelve cousins milling about.

It was also unusual for the telephone to ring at 10:30 on New Year's Eve, as most people wait until midnight. Richard Anderson, Dixie's dad, was calling. One of his young cows was trying to have her first calf and was in trouble. Could Bill and his brothers come help?

My brother Art and I swung into Bill's pickup and we were quickly on our way to Richard's farm.

In the hay shed, next to the dairy barn, we found Richard with the heifer trying to birth her first calf. She was still on her feet, exhausted from laboring for a day in what we soon learned was a breech birth position. We don't think of cows having facial expressions, but there was pain and fear in this animal's eyes as she went down on her side, panting.

It was already too late to get a veterinarian to the farm to save the lives of the young mother and her calf. Whatever had to happen had to happen quickly. Hot water and soap is the one staple everyone knows to have at hand in a home birth situation. With a five-gallon bucket of scalding water and a bar of Ivory Soap at hand, Bill quickly took off his coat and shirt, lathered up his arm and plunged, arm-deep into the birth canal.

He felt around for a few seconds then told us the calf is turned sideways and the only way it will come out is if he can turn it. But it would come out of the birth canal backwards. In a few minutes, he guided the rear feet into the open. Then he looped a rope around both feet. With both Art and I pulling and Bill guiding, we soon had the calf free of its mother.

Bill quickly realized the calf was not breathing. The backwards delivery had forced the calf's internal organs into its chest and were compressing its lungs. Massaging the chest restored the organs to their proper positions. After a couple of CPR compressions, Bill gave the calf the breath of life. Soon the calf began breathing and was up on all fours, looking for milk.

It felt warmer in that frigid hay shed as the new mother licked her baby dry and prepared for the first feeding. Bill washed and dried and shrugged back into his heavy flannel shirt and woolen coat. A new life. A new year.

# Color Theory

In physics, red, green and blue provide the base for the thousands of colors the human eye can perceive. Each color has a wavelength range and they're measured in nanometers — one-billionth of a meter. Red emits at 610 to 780 nanometers, green at 500 to 570nm and blue at 450 to 500nm. The human eye receives these various signals, and the brain translates them into visible colors.

Mom was the daughter of an Advent Christian minister who forbade her to wear or possess anything red. As red generates excitement in the higher wavelength, he considered it to be sinful and inappropriate for a Christian young lady.

It's a foregone conclusion that red would be her favorite color. She was ecstatic when Dad came home in a brand new red 1948 Ford pickup truck. Fourteen years later, she gleefully co-signed the finance papers for my red 1955 Thunderbird. Often her Christmas present to Dad would be a cardinal red, hand-knitted sweater vest.

As a child, my favorite color was green. It was inevitable being raised on a farm and surrounded by the lush, leafy green of the hardwoods, the rich verdant green of the pine and fir trees, the tender green of emerging corn fields growing in to the silvery green of the maturing stalks and fading into the yellow green after the harvest. The hayfields progressed through a similar metamorphosis as the light green immature grass emerged, grew and darkened into maturity, then muted as the seed heads diluted the richness and the breezes rippled the display into a multi-hued palette.

I've logged many hours in the air, preoccupied with cloud cover and clear skies. Later, I owned a boat and became more involved with Casco Bay and the nearby lakes. It seems natural that my favorite color has moved from the green of my youth to the less-hurried blue wavelength of my more mature years.

# The Gift

One summer Sunday afternoon, Nancy and I were on a cruise on board my customer Bob Berger's boat, the Mary Ann. I had recently done over five thousand dollars' worth of repairs and updates to this 27-foot North Sea Trawler's engine and driveline, and knew the boat was in excellent condition, and her hull sound. I also knew I could never afford to own one like it.

When I first met Bob, he and his wife Mary Ann, a slight woman with crippling arthritis, lived in Texas where they ran a large day care facility. They liked to summer in South Freeport in a cottage they had renovated into a year-round home overlooking the harbor. Eventually they left Texas and made South Freeport their permanent home.

During the ten years I had maintained Bob's boats, I got to know him as a kind man with many interests. He was tall, slightly stooped, with unruly hair, mischievous brown eyes, and a love of bacon. He made a point of being unorthodox despite his strict Jewish upbringing.

On that sunny day I was staring out to the bay, mesmerized by the sun reflecting off the water. Bob motioned for me to join him in the cabin where he stood at the helm. I wondered if he noticed a strange sound in the engine, if there was something I needed to fix.

"When this boat comes out of the water this fall, it is going to your house."

I figured he might want me to store the Mary Ann and perhaps do some work on it.

"No, I want you to have it. I am getting old and I don't feel I can operate and maintain it anymore. I will sell you the boat for one dollar and my only stipulation is that when you decide to stop boating, you will pass it along."

Of course I accepted. A few days later, I met Bob at his bank where, in front of the notary public, we signed papers and I handed Bob a single dollar bill. We shook hands on the agreement that I would pass the boat on when I was through boating.

Bob's wife Mary Ann passed away a while before he handed the boat to me, and I wondered if gifting the boat was his way of letting go. Later I learned that Bob's doctor had diagnosed him with terminal liver disease and Bob knew his days were numbered.

Out of respect for Bob and as a tribute to his wife, we kept the white, cursive name of Mary Ann on the boat's bright blue stern.

Mary Ann changed our lives. The following spring we joined the Centerboard Yacht Club where we moored the boat and broadened our circle of acquaintances, friends and potential customers now that I had become a boat engine mechanic.

An English boat designed for the North Sea, Mary Ann's over-sized rudder made her very easy to maneuver. With tall sides, there was less chance of grandchildren falling overboard. She was slow and lumbering, with a top speed of 18 knots or about 21 miles an hour. Normal cruise was about 12 knots, fast enough to get where you wanted, but slow enough to notice curious seals popping their heads out of the water.

We had lived on the coast for over forty years, and now suddenly Casco Bay was our playground. We spent part of every good weather weekend from early May until early November on the Mary Ann. Sometimes it was just Nancy and me and a picnic lunch anchored in a cove somewhere on a Sunday afternoon reading the newspaper — with a gentle breeze, no mosquitoes, and a rocking motion essential for good napping.

Many boating adventures included our entire family — my son, Richard, his wife Michelle and their two sons, Riley and Tate, and my daughter Carolyn, her husband Cal and their two sons, Aidan and Max. Overwhelmed with eager deckhands, we would circle Casco Bay, find a place to anchor and spread a picnic lunch on the engine cover. We would cruise to Eagle Island and tour Admiral Peary's home. Sometimes we'd go to Peaks Island for a meal at one of the several restaurants or make a run up toward Cousins Island to watch the seals bask on the ledges. We often circled around Long Island and made our way to Shark Cove where we'd anchor in the beautiful sheltered bay where the sun always seemed to shine on its uncrowded white sand beach.

Eventually we ran out of places to go, and alternative places were further than we wanted to travel. After two seasons of using the boat only a few times, we decided owning Mary Ann didn't justify the $3000.00 it cost to keep her moored. That brought up a quandary, however. I had promised to pass the boat on if I gave up boating.

We had owned the boat almost ten years and developed many boating friendships both in and out of the yacht club. I realized if I gave the boat to one friend, it wouldn't be fair to other friends. I solved this problem by selling the boat for best offer and donating the proceeds to the Hot Tub Replacement committee at the South Portland Recreation Center.

The fellow who bought the Mary Ann wrote a check to the committee and when the boat went into the water the next spring he changed the name on the stern from Mary Ann to Hot Tub.

The story almost ends there. About three months after we sold Mary Ann, a man whom I had never met called and asked if I would like to take his 1974 23-foot Chris-Craft Lancer for one dollar. He was moving to the Midwest and couldn't justify the cost of moving it. I kept it for a year, did some deferred maintenance, and sold it for sixty percent more than I got for the Mary Ann.

I guess you could say gifts have a way of passing themselves on.

# Acknowledgments

This book did not get produced by my hand alone. In fact, the fingerprints of several people are all over it.

First, I thank my wife, Nancy, for encouraging me to join her writing group. Without that first step, I would not have written these stories. I also thank our writing coach, Judith Hannemann, whose guidance has kept our tight-knit, enthusiastic group of writers at the Dempsey Center in South Portland, Maine, writing for many years.

Last but not least, I'd like to thank my daughter Carolyn for believing my words are worthy enough to typeset and publish.

# Tales from the Hayloft Family Album

John and Arthur Harris, Labor Day Picnic, Ferry Beach, 1940

Art, Jim and Bill, 1945

Bill, Jim, Art 1946

Alton Bay, New Hampshire, 1948 : Ruth, John, Jim, Art & Bill

Winching Dad's tractor from Round Pond, 1953

Bill, Jim, Art 1955

Suzy, A Real Cow Dog

Harris Farm, 1957

Jim's '55 Thunderbird at Harris Farm, 1962

My soon-to-be-forever-co-pilot, Nancy. Niagara Falls, 1964

Nancy and our 1941 Taylorcraft

Nancy at Harris Farm

Carolyn, Richard & Nancy. Houlton, Maine 1972

Jim and the Mary Ann, Centerboard Yacht Club, South Portland, 2012

Jim & Cal (Carolyn's husband) at The Engine Room, South Portland, 2012

Fisherman's Point, South Portland, overlooking Casco Bay